Alice Walker:

The Color Purple and Other Works

∞Writers and Their Works∞

Alice Walker:
The Color Purple and Other Works

MARY DONNELLY

Marshall Cavendish
Benchmark
New York

Special thanks to Judith Musser, associate professor of English and American Studies at LaSalle University in Pennsylvania, for her expert review of this manuscript.

Marshall Cavendish Benchmark
99 White Plains Road
Tarrytown, NY 10591
www.marshallcavendish.us

Library of Congress Cataloging-in-Publication Data

Donnelly, Mary.
Alice Walker : The color purple and other works / by Mary Donnelly.
p. cm. — (Writers and their works)
Includes bibliographical references and index.
Summary: "A biography of writer Alice Walker that describes her era, her major work—The Color Purple, her life, and the legacy of her writing"—Provided by publisher.
ISBN 978-0-7614-4281-3
1. Walker, Alice, 1944–2. African American women authors—20th century—Biography. I. Title.
PS3573.A425Z635 2009
813'.54—dc22
[B]
2008050263

Publisher: Michelle Bisson
Art Director: Anahid Hamparian
Series Designer: Sonia Chagbatzanian

The photographs in this book are used by permission and through the courtesy of:
Noah Berger/AP Images: cover, 2; Judith Sullivan/Getty Images: 6; The Granger Collection: 16; Frazer Harrison/Getty Images: 18; Robert Kelley/Time Life Pictures/Getty Images: 23; © 1977 Christopher R. Harris: 27; Bettmann/Corbis: 34, 57; Petr Kramer/Getty Images: 42; Baron Sekiya/The New York Times/Redux: 45; Hulton Archive/Getty Images: 48, 65; AP Images/Bill Hudson: 54; Francis Miller/Time & Life Pictures/Getty Images: 58; Warner Bros/The Kobal Collection: 72, 76, 87, 90, 106; Photofest: 78; Cover, The Third Life of Grange Copeland, © 1970 by Alice Walker. A Harvest book, Harcourt, Inc. Cover photo © Corbis: 108; Cover, Meridian, © 1976 by Alice Walker, afterword © 1988 by Alice Walker. A Harvest book, Harcourt, Inc. Cover photo © LWA-Stephen Welstead/Corbis: 113; Cover, Everyday Use by Alice Walker, Women Writers series, edited by Barbara T. Christian. ©1994 by Rutgers University Press. Cover photo ©1991 by Jean Weisinger: 125

Photo research by Lindsay Aveilhe and Linda Sykes,
Linda Sykes Picture Research Inc., Hilton Head, SC

Printed in Malaysia
1 3 5 6 4 2

Contents

ALICE WALKER HAS ACHIEVED BOTH FAME AND CRITICAL APPLAUSE THROUGHOUT HER CAREER. IN 2006, SHE WAS INDUCTED INTO THE CALIFORNIA HALL OF FAME, ALONG WITH ACHIEVERS SUCH AS CESAR CHAVEZ, RONALD REAGAN, AND BILLIE JEAN KING.

Introduction

ALICE WALKER consistently ranks among the greatest
American writers of the twentieth century. Through her
novels, short stories, poetry, and essays, she outlines many
important issues concerning the effect of authoritarian
thinking upon its often innocent victims, and the possibility of meaningful, productive resistance.

Walker's work gives a voice to those that have no
voice: usually, though not always, poor, rural black
women. Robbed of power and the right to make decisions
about their own lives by a range of forces standing against
them—their religious leaders; a brutal economic system;
racial prejudice, which is often encoded into law; and the
frequent misogyny of the men with whom they choose or
are forced to share their lives—Walker's heroines nevertheless articulate clear visions not just of the wrongs they
face, but also of the hope and strength that cannot be
quenched within them. Not every Walker heroine works
up the courage to say, as Celie in *The Color Purple* does
to her abusive husband Mr. _____, "You a lowdown dog
is what's wrong. . . . It's time to leave you and enter into
the Creation. And your dead body just the welcome mat I
need" (199). Most, however, do develop the ability to
stand up for themselves in acts of small or large resistance,
whether refusing to give a quilt to a condescending child,
as in "Everyday Use," or murdering those who would
continue the disturbing and violent tradition of female
genital mutilation, as in *Possessing the Secret of Joy*.
Clearly there are many ways of formulating resistance in
these texts.

This process of identifying and celebrating resistance plays a central role in Walker's larger project: recognizing the value and individuality of each person, the distinct patterns of experience and soul that mark each person as valuable.

Along with this, Walker provides a mystical view of nature, identifying from her earliest works a sense of what the eighteenth-century Romantics would call the sublime: exceeding sensory perception and rational thought, nature becomes a force, a character in its own right, with a soul, and with whom characters can have rich, fulfilling relationships. When Meridian Hill in Walker's novel *Meridian* discovers the ancient Cherokee shrine known as the Sacred Serpent Mound on her farm and encounters something like religious ecstasy there, when Shug Avery points out the beauty of the color purple in nature, we can see that Walker is pointing us toward an intense connection between nature, spirituality, and identity.

Walker's first book of nonfiction, entitled *In Search of Our Mothers' Gardens*, suggests this connection. In the title essay, she argues passionately that her own mother's creative spark was expressed via nature: She was a passionate gardener, and she threw all of her soul into her flower garden: "I notice that it is only when my mother is working in her flowers that she is radiant, almost to the point of being invisible—except as Creator: hand and eye. She is involved in work her soul must have. Ordering the universe in her personal conception of beauty" (241). Thus, although it is possible to discuss aspects of Walker's work, such as resistance, humanism, spirituality, nature, and womanism (her own term for the black feminism she practices), it is an injustice to her work to attempt to separate these strands of meaning. The strength of her work lies in the interweaving of her concerns, her absolute insistence that all persons and the natural world want and demand justice. She is a passionate and gifted advocate for their cause.

Part I:
Walker's Life

panties you got on." Just as quick as that, Miss Shug turned loose, let 'em drop to the ground, and with her foot flipped panties over to Ma-Ma, who put them in her pocket. My grandmother looked over and said, "Ooh, give me them pretty panties you got on."

Just as quick as that, Miss Shug turned loose, let 'em drop to the ground, and with her foot flipped panties over to Ma-Ma, who put them in her pocket. My grandmother looked over and said, "Ooh, give me them pretty panties you got on." Just as quick as that, Miss Shug turned loose, let 'em drop to the ground, and with her foot flipped panties over to Ma-Ma, who put them in her pocket. My grandmother looked over and said, "Ooh, give me them pretty panties you got on." Just as quick as that, Miss Shug turned loose, let 'em drop to the ground, and with her foot flipped panties over to Ma-Ma, who put them in her pocket. My grandmother looked over and said, "Ooh, give me them pretty panties you got on." Just as quick as that, Miss Shug turned loose, let 'em drop to the ground, and with her foot flipped panties over to Ma-Ma, who put them in her pocket. My grandmother looked over and said, "Ooh, give me them pretty panties you got on." Just as quick as that, Miss Shug turned loose, let 'em drop to the ground, and with her foot flipped panties over to Ma-Ma, who put them in her pocket. My grandmother looked over and said, "Ooh, give me them pretty panties you got on." Just as quick as that, Miss Shug turned loose, let 'em drop to the ground, and with her foot flipped panties over to Ma-Ma, who put them in her pocket. My grandmother looked over and said, "Ooh, give me them pretty panties you got on." Just as quick as that, Miss Shug turned loose, let 'em drop to the ground, and with her foot flipped panties over to Ma-Ma, who put them in her pocket. My grandmother looked over and said, "Ooh, give me them pretty panties you got on." Just as quick as that, Miss Shug turned loose, let 'em drop to the ground, and with her foot flipped panties over to Ma-Ma, who put them in her pocket. My grandmother looked over and said, "Ooh, give me them pretty panties you got on." Just as quick as that, Miss Shug turned loose, let 'em drop to the ground, and with her foot flipped

Chapter 1

A Brief Biography of Alice Walker

Early Childhood

Alice Malsenior Walker was born on February 9, 1944, in Eatonton, Georgia, the last of eight children. Her father, Willie Lee Walker, was a sharecropper, someone who lived on and farmed another person's land, with some of the produce or financial proceeds going to the landlord as rent. Sharecropping was a common way for the poor to make a living in the rural South, but it was practically impossible to get ahead financially.

Alice Walker's mother, Minnie Tallulah Walker (born Grant), was a stay-at-home mother and an avid gardener and quilter. These activities can be found throughout her daughter's work, whether it is through an appreciation of the mystical qualities of nature or a solid appreciation of quilting. As Walker noted: "I just feel really good and protected and blessed . . . when I am under quilts made by my mother. . . . It's the same tradition as painting or carving. . . . The power is partly about grounding yourself in something that is humble . . . something you can see take form through your own effort" (Freeman, cited in White 57).

Walker's early life was spent in great poverty, but her supportive and loving parents made sure that none of their children would be handicapped by a lack of financial resources. Alice herself was very bright, an early reader, and quite self-possessed. Her teachers remember her as being one of their most memorable students. In Walker's essay "Beauty: When the Other Dancer is the Self," she describes her childhood self. Walker draws a picture of herself as a perfect little girl, reciting an Easter speech in her best dress, proud and confident. As she rises to give her speech, she radiates maturity, poise, and an indefinable spirit:

> When I rise to give my speech I do so on a great wave of love and pride and expectation. People in the church stop rustling their new crinolines. They seem to hold their breath. I can tell they admire my dress, but it is my spirit, bordering on sassiness (womanishness), they secretly applaud.
>
> "That girl's a little *mess*," they whisper to each other, pleased. ("Beauty," 385)

"Mess" in this context is a compliment indicating her precocious intelligence and bearing, something Walker clearly prized. Nevertheless, this undoubtedly idealized memory sets the stage for a tragic fall.

Trauma

Walker was only eight when a simple childhood accident forever changed the way she saw herself and the world. She was a tomboy, and played cowboys and Indians regularly with two of her older brothers. They had matching outfits and were armed with bows and arrows.

Neither age nor gender stopped her: She could keep up with the boys, until one day her parents bought a gift for her brothers that they did not buy for her: air rifles that used BBs (solid metal balls about one-eighth of an inch in diameter) as shot. And she, as a girl, describes herself as "instantly . . . relegated to the position of Indian." ("Beauty" 386) On top of a garage roof, she was shot with a BB, which lodged in the tissue of her eye. Her brothers, panicked about being caught and punished, convinced her to lie to their parents, telling them that she had stepped on barbed wire. Of course, had that been the source of her injury, she would not have had a foreign object in her eye. This lie led to a dangerous delay in treating the wound.

Her parents did not have a car, and a white motorist refused to pick up her father when he tried to take her to the hospital. She was treated at home with folk medicine, in an attempt to control her fever and infection, rather than dealing with the injury itself. After a week, she had lost the sight in that eye, so it was clear that the medicine wasn't effective. Her parents took her to a doctor who terrified Alice by warning her about "sympathetic blindness"—that is, he told her that she might also lose sight in her other eye.

In Walker's biography, her brother Curtis tells the story somewhat differently. In his narrative, Alice was not unarmed. "She had Bobby's gun. I had mine. I shot my gun and the BB rose high in the air and hit her right smack in the eye. It was a terrible accident, no doubt about it. And as far as the outcome, it doesn't make a bit of difference, but Alice had a BB gun, too" (White 35). Their brother Bobby confirms this version of the story.

Whether or not Alice was armed, the injury had far-reaching and harmful effects. She lost her sight in one eye and developed an unsightly blob of whitish scar tissue on the eye. But the effect on her perception of herself was worse than the vision loss.

From a confident girl who was afraid of nothing, Walker became shy and introverted. It did not help that the family moved that summer, putting her in a new school and pulling her away from friends and teachers who had known Alice before the accident. Realizing that their mistake had worsened the trauma, her parents hastily sent Alice back to live with her grandmother, which Alice interpreted as rejection. "Alice said she felt both abandoned and punished by her parents' decision to send her away from home. . . . Ashamed of her appearance and unable to understand why she was 'exiled,' her brothers left to run free, Alice became increasingly despondent and withdrawn. She took refuge in the books she received from friends and relatives at Christmas and for birthdays—*Gulliver's Travels, Robinson Crusoe,* and collections of fairy tales. She also began to write sad poems"(White 39–40). Reading and writing became a refuge for Walker at a very painful time.

Surgery and Rejuvenation

Alice was fourteen in the summer of 1958 when her brother Bill, who was living in Boston, invited her to spend the summer with him, his wife, and their newborn son. Officially Alice was to spend the summer as a mother's helper. But the real reason for the invitation was much more direct: Bill, who had paid for the medical treatment Alice had received in Georgia, now wanted to do something else for his little sister by bringing her to a major city with more competent medical care than had been available in their small Georgia town. Without telling Alice where they were going or why, he brought her to the Eye and Ear Infirmary at Massachusetts General Hospital, which was affiliated with Harvard Medical School (White, 45). Because Bill was her brother and not her parent, he could not authorize her treatment, and there was a slight delay, but by early August, Alice was ready for surgery to have the scar tissue in her eye removed.

The surgery itself was unproblematic. There was no way to restore sight to the eye, but the surgeon, Morriss Henry (whom Alice remembered by calling him "O. Henry," after the author) removed the white tissue that affected Alice's appearance. That relatively minor change in her appearance rejuvenated Alice's sense of self. In her words:

> Almost immediately I become a different person from the girl who does not raise her head. Or so I think. Now that I've raised my head I win the

boyfriend of my dreams. Now that I've raised my head I have plenty of friends. Now that I've raised my head classwork comes from my lips as fault-lessly as Easter speeches did, and I leave high school as valedictorian, most popular student, and queen, hardly believing my luck. ("Beauty," 390)

Walker, whose grades had suffered during the six years she had the scar, did well in high school, and got a scholarship allowing her to attend Spelman College, an institution founded to educate young black women, in the fall of 1961.

Life at Spelman College

As Walker headed to college, her sense of justice was offended when she was asked to move to the back of the bus taking her to Atlanta (White, 64–65). This request was a common occurrence in the Jim Crow South, even after Rosa Parks and the Montgomery Bus Boycott of 1955–1956. Nevertheless it upset Walker to be so bla-tantly disrespected, and she arrived in Atlanta with a dual sense of purpose: not just to pursue her education, but to take part in the civil rights movement as well.

But Spelman in the early 1960s did not educate young women to be activists. It educated them to be good Christian wives and mothers, to conduct themselves like ladies, and always to retain their dignity. The civil rights movement was in full swing in the streets of Atlanta, but, as Howard Zinn—one of Walker's professors—noted, the young women of Spelman "were expected to dress a cer-tain way, walk a certain way, pour tea a certain way. There was compulsory chapel six times a week. Students had to sign in and out of their dormitories, and be in by 10:00 pm. Their contacts with men were carefully moni-tored; the college authorities were determined to counter stories of the sexually free black woman and worse, the

WHEN ROSA PARKS WAS ARRESTED FOR REFUSING TO SIT IN THE BACK OF A BUS (*HERE SHE IS BEING FINGERPRINTED BY A POLICE OFFICER AFTER HER ARREST*), SHE INSPIRED A GENERATION, OF WHOM ALICE WALKER TOOK AN ARDENT PART.

pregnant, unmarried black girl" (Zinn 18–19). Academics were a serious business at Spelman, but Walker was not interested in attending finishing school. This was Atlanta, 1961, and in the opinion of Walker and many people like her, there were more important things to do than learn to behave like a lady.

The People's Historian

Walker found a kindred spirit in her history professor, noted leftist intellectual Howard Zinn. He was, Walker remembers, "the first white man with whom she'd ever had a real conversation" (White 69). He felt strongly the injustices of segregation. "Both on the Spelman campus and in the often surreal, segregated world of Atlanta, Professor Zinn, attentive and always bearing a warm and welcoming smile, stood in unshakable solidarity with black people" (White 69). Zinn, the author of the populist classic *A People's History of the United States*, brought his concern with injustice and liberty to his work at Spelman. He was particularly taken with young Walker: "I remember my first impression of her: small, slender but strong-looking, smooth brown skin, one eye silent, the other doubly inquiring with a hint of laughter. Her manner was polite, but not in the directed way of a 'Spelman girl,' rather almost ironically polite. Not disrespectful, simply confident" (Zinn 44). Zinn inspired students in the Social Science Club he advised and encouraged their dedication to social justice. He was also in favor of their rebellions against the restrictions imposed by their college.

Zinn's encouragement of student resistance did not go unnoticed, and he was considered rabble-rousing by his superiors. "[Spelman president Albert] Manley considered Zinn . . . the prime 'instigator' of the growing discontent Spelman women were voicing about the administration's paternalism, conservatism, and ongoing efforts to restrict their involvement in civil rights protests" (White 79). To be fair, the administration was conducting itself as it had always been forced to: the way that had been necessary under Jim Crow. Educating young black women was unusual enough; should Spelman students become active in the civil rights movement, the college itself could be at risk. As Howard Zinn noted, "It was as if there was an unwritten, unspoken agreement between the white power

HOWARD ZINN'S *PEOPLE'S HISTORY OF THE UNITED STATES* LOOKED AT THE NATION'S HISTORY THROUGH THE EYES OF THOSE TRADITIONALLY OVERLOOKED; THOSE AT THE BOTTOM. AS WALKER'S PROFESSOR AT SPELMAN COLLEGE, HE FUELED HER CONCERN FOR SOCIAL JUSTICE.

structure of Atlanta and the administrations of the black colleges: We white folk will let you colored folk have your nice little college. You can educate your colored girls to [be of] service to the Negro community, to become teachers and social workers, maybe even doctors and lawyers. We won't bother you. . . . This pact was symbolized by a twelve-foot-high stone fence around the campus. . ." (19).

Still, it was not a time for safe choices, in the opinion of many students and faculty. Acceding to the cultural demands of another era in the heated environment of the day was seen as a passive acceptance of the very inequalities that the civil rights movement was determined to address. Neither the activists nor the administration was willing to back down. However, power—at least within the college—was not equally distributed, and Zinn was dismissed in the summer of 1963, while the students were away. When this happened, Walker herself was staying with her brother in Boston, far from the heated streets of Atlanta.

Walker spent much of the summer of 1963 with David DeMoss, whom she had met when he was an exchange student at Morehouse College and she was at Spelman. Their relationship was complicated by the fact that DeMoss was white. Interracial relationships were rare in the United States at that time, and neither family nor strangers were happy about it. The young couple was aware of but blissfully unconcerned about the potential problems their relationship might face because of their differences. Together they attended the August 1963 March on Washington, featuring Martin Luther King Jr.'s groundbreaking "I Have a Dream" speech.

But the news of Zinn's dismissal cast a shadow over this blissful summer. She wrote to Zinn to express her dismay, noting that "I've tried to imagine Spelman without you—and I can't at all" (White 80). When she returned to Spelman in the fall, she continued to advocate for her former professor in the Spelman student newspaper, *The Spotlight*.

> I am not sorry for Zinn in the usual sense of the word, the world takes care of its own and history favors great men—the more injustices overcome and profited from, the greater the personality. I am sorry though for us, as a group of presumably mature and civilized individuals, that we can settle down to "business as usual" with only a second thought to what we have lost and what we have become. (White, 87)

The letter caused a storm of controversy, evidence of how even gentle criticism of the school could create a crisis. Walker, already feeling uncomfortable at Spelman, began to think about transferring to another college.

One of her other history professors, Staughton Lynd, was the son of a professor at Sarah Lawrence College in Bronxville, New York. Lynd, realizing more than Walker did how difficult her public support for Zinn would make her life at Spelman, contacted his mother about the possibility of Walker going to school there. Walker's strong academic record and her political activism were points in her favor for attending Sarah Lawrence. She received a full scholarship, and moved north for the spring semester of 1964.

Sarah Lawrence College

Sarah Lawrence College could hardly have been more different from Spelman. At Spelman, Walker had been surrounded primarily by the daughters of the black middle class who were separated from her by economic status, but not by race or significant cultural and regional differences. But Sarah Lawrence was radically different. Bronxville, New York, only a short distance from New York City, was cold and foreign: an alien world. Walker's classmates were the daughters of wealth and privilege, overwhelmingly white, with whom the daughter of black sharecroppers shared little common ground.

But Walker was at Sarah Lawrence to continue her education and become a writer, and in that sense, she did very well. She became the student of noted American poet Muriel Rukeyser, who, as a young woman, had walked away from the expectations of her own privileged upbringing to report on the Scottsboro Boys and the Spanish Civil War, one of the first serious battles against fascism in Europe, during the mid–1930s. (The Scottsboro Boys were a group of nine black youths from Alabama who were falsely convicted of the rape of two white women. Their 1931 case was a symbol of all that was wrong with Jim Crow justice.) Both assignments would have been highly unusual for a wealthy young woman.

Rukeyser believed that poetry was a valid form of activism, a perspective that had a deep impact on young Walker, who was already attuned to the connection between her art and the world around her. As Walker notes, "she taught me that it was possible to be passion-ate about writing and to live in the world on your own terms" (White, 109). And Rukeyser, for her part, recog-nized in the young Walker a true writer's vocation, and fostered it wherever possible. She called Walker "a stu-dent of remarkable capacities" and expected great things from her, an expectation that Walker herself took seriously.

After her second year at Sarah Lawrence, Walker returned to the South in the summer of 1965 to partici-pate in voter registration. Though blacks in the South the-oretically had the right to vote, they were often prevented from doing so by unfriendly landlords and defiant law enforcement. Potential voters, as well as those who vol-unteered to help them exercise their rights, like Walker, often faced violent opposition. "As those rocks and bottles whizzed past my head, I realized I could easily lose the sight in my other eye. There was no support for us in that community and I wasn't ready to be a martyr just then" (White, 110). Instead she went to Africa.

In Kenya, Walker worked in pineapple fields and helped build a school, but the crushing ill health and poverty of the native Africans dismayed her. At that time much of Africa was newly decolonized, but the promises of decolonization—a restoration of national sovereignty and prosperity—were as distant as ever, and the people, sick and malnourished, were left to deal with the scars of colonial occupation—ravaged, overcultivated land and polluted water—often still under the control of European corporations, with little broader support. After her stint in Kenya, Walker went to Uganda, where she unexpectedly encountered her old Boston boyfriend, David DeMoss, who was working with the Peace Corps.

Walker was delighted to see DeMoss in Africa in 1965, and they connected there, far from home. Although they had been diligent about birth control during their earlier relationship, this encounter was unexpected and unprotected. The result was an unwelcome and problematic situation: Walker returned to the United States and her last semester of Sarah Lawrence pregnant.

Before the Supreme Court's 1973 decision in *Roe* v. *Wade*, terminating an unwanted pregnancy was illegal in the United States unless the health of the mother was deemed to be at stake. In addition to the legal problems, an unmarried pregnant woman faced social stigmas and real problems, such as expulsion from school for moral grounds. Walker depended on her scholarship to finish school. She could not marry DeMoss, and even if she had married him, it would have meant the end of her education. Walker knew that this meant she would be forced into the life of hard work, drudgery, and poverty she had fought so hard to escape. In the face of these unacceptable options, Walker decided to pursue the risky path of seeking an illegal abortion.

WHEN HE RAN FOR PRESIDENT IN 1960, JOHN F. KENNEDY FAMOUSLY SAID, "ASK NOT WHAT YOUR COUNTRY CAN DO FOR YOU, BUT WHAT YOU CAN DO FOR YOUR COUNTRY." MANY YOUNG PEOPLE, INCLUDING THOSE PICTURED HERE, DECIDED TO JOIN THE PEACE CORPS, WHICH HELPED POOR PEOPLE ALL OVER THE WORLD, PARTICULARLY IN AFRICA.

However, Walker didn't know any doctors who would perform the procedure, and she had no money to pay a doctor even she could find one. She sank into depression, telling only a few close friends and her sisters Mamie and Ruth that she was pregnant. Ruth, who was unable to bear children, encouraged her sister to have the baby and give it to her. Mamie, unmarried, was openly critical of her younger sister's sexual activity. Walker was determined to keep the news of her pregnancy from the rest of her family. Her depression worsened as the pregnancy progressed: She stopped eating and seriously considered suicide, a death she felt her family would accept once they learned of her condition.

Abortion is a relatively simple procedure if performed by a trained physician during early pregnancy, but the chance for complication increases with the length of the pregnancy. Time, then, was of the essence, particularly given Walker's depression and suicidal thoughts. Her friends at college, who could see both the bright future in front of her and her growing abdomen, struggled to help her find an answer, to literally save her life. One friend located a doctor in Manhattan who would perform an abortion. It would cost $2,000 (approximately $12,000 in current dollars), an unthinkable amount of money for a scholarship student to raise in the mid–1960s. Walker did not have the cash, so she asked for help from her friends, who worked together to come up with the money. DeMoss, still in the Peace Corps, sent what he could, too. In the end she was able to afford the abortion, but her anger at a system that forced women into such desperate straits remained. In an interview several years later, Walker said, "Society accused us of being sinful, shameful, and criminal for wanting to have abortions. The way I see it, the 'crime' was that doctors could get away with profiting off our tremendous need" (O'Brien, 188). Her experience led Walker to become a prominent and vocal supporter of abortion rights.

The abortion had another important effect on young Walker: In its aftermath, she produced reams of poetry that she handed off, almost without caring what became of it, to her writing professor Muriel Rukeyser. Rukeyser showed the poetry to agents and tried to help her young student publish her work. By the time Walker graduated from Sarah Lawrence in January 1966, she was well on her way to doing so. Her story "To Hell with Dying," an affirmation of the value of life and art, was also composed during this period, and in 1967, black author and Harlem Renaissance leader Langston Hughes included it in his anthology *The Best Short Stories by Negro Writers*, making it Walker's first published prose.

New York City

After graduation Walker followed the path of many other young artists and moved to the Lower East Side of New York City. The countercultural and anti–establishment political movement that would dominate American cultural life for the next several years was already in full swing in New York. Walker's political beliefs led her to take a job helping people on welfare navigate New York City's massive Social Services Department. "It's what most of the writers, dancers, painters, and other artists did back then. . . . We were all radical movement people who wanted to save the world. We believed that working for the welfare department would give us a chance to help people" (White, 122). Through her job, Walker saw first-hand the effect of poverty on the urban residents whose cases she handled. She connected it with her own rural sharecropping background, and used the link in her first novel, *The Third Life of Grange Copeland*, in which madness and violence in the rural South and the urban North are intimately interrelated as a result of racial and economic injustice.

Meanwhile, Muriel Rukeyser's agent, Monica McCall, was sending out the manuscript of Walker's poems, called *Once*, to publishers. Walker was largely unaware of this development. "Muriel gave the poems to Monica; I didn't have anything to do with it. . . . I had needed to write them, but I didn't care if they ever got published. That was irrelevant to me" (White, 127). In the meantime, she worked full-time, wrote, and dated a number of men, including an old friend from her Spelman days, Robert Allen, now a graduate student in New York. The grind of being a caseworker was beginning to wear on her, however, and she feared that her creative gifts would dry up if she continued to pursue her current path. After only six months, she resigned from the welfare department.

While she had been a student at Spelman, Walker had turned down an offer to study in Europe funded by Charles Merrill, the cofounder of the financial firm Merrill Lynch, angrily noting that for black Americans, Europe was not, in fact, the "cradle of civilization." Walker believed that the attempt to instill its values in young black Americans represented another kind of colonization, a forced reassignment of identifications from the African slave experience to the white Europeans who had enslaved them. Charles Merrill once again approached her, this time offering to fund a trip to Africa. Walker initially accepted, planning to go to Senegal, but again, events intervened, and in the heated summer of 1966, she reconsidered: "What was the point of studying French in Senegal, she asked herself, when black parents in Biloxi and Tuskegee couldn't vote, when their children were given secondhand books (if any) from white schools inscribed with 'Nigger' and 'Long Live the Klan'? None that she could tell"(White, 130). For the second time, Walker saw Merrill's largesse as standing between her and her own people. Instead of going to Africa, Walker packed up and began to work with the National Association for the Advancement of Colored People's (NAACP) Legal Defense and Educational Fund. It proved to be one of the most crucial decisions of her life.

Mel Leventhal

Mississippi was, in many ways, the center of the civil rights movement. Although Jim Crow laws enforcing racial segregation held sway throughout the South, they were rarely enforced with as much zest and violence as in Mississippi. Emmett Till, a young teenager accused of flirting with a white woman, was killed in Mississippi. Medgar Evers, an NAACP field secretary who organized protests against segregated businesses, was murdered on his own doorstep, holding a box of T-shirts that said: "Jim Crow Must Go." And, as recently as two years before

AFTER COLLEGE, WALKER MOVED TO MISSISSIPPI TO TAKE PART IN THE CIVIL RIGHTS MOVEMENT OF THE EARLY 1960s. IT WAS THERE THAT SHE MET MEL LEVENTHAL, WHO WOULD BECOME THE FATHER OF HER ONLY CHILD.

Walker's arrival, three civil rights workers (two of them white) had been killed by local residents, including the county sheriff. Clearly it was no place for a young, educated black woman. But the very things that made Mississippi so terrifying drew Walker, who saw an opportunity there to do some real good for people who actually needed her.

Her fate, however, lay in Mississippi in more ways than one. She was working for Marian Wright, later Edelman, who was at that time head of the NAACP Legal Defense Fund, and would later found the Children's Defense Fund and cowrite the book *It Takes a Village* with Hillary Clinton. She became a powerful mentor for young Walker. But the very first thing that Walker did in Mississippi was go to lunch with her new colleague, a young law student from New York named Melvyn Leventhal, then in his second summer of work with the NAACP in Mississippi.

Walker had expected that her work would involve registering voters, as it had the summer before. But because of her excellent writing skills, she was assigned to help take the depositions, or legal statements to be used as evidence, of blacks in Greenwood, Mississippi, who had been evicted from their homes for registering to vote (thereby voiding their registrations, since voting districts are tied to residency). She became part of a two-person team with Leventhal.

They drove together to Greenwood, about 90 miles from Jackson, where the central office was located. There they checked into a hotel, newly desegregated after the Civil Rights Act of 1964 had banned segregated accommodations. (In *The Color Purple*, Shug Avery notes that she and her husband had to drive all night because they could not find a hotel that would allow them to stay (108). Although Walker and Leventhal had separate rooms, they were concerned enough about the openly hostile reception from the clerk that they decided to room together, fearing an attack from local racists. They didn't sleep, but spent the night sitting up in separate beds, reading to one another all night from the Bible, specifically from the highly erotic Song of Solomon.

No attack came that night, though the two became fast friends. The following day, however, they were warned not to spend another night in Greenwood. When they left, a truck followed them suspiciously closely as they headed back to the highway and Jackson. Just as they were starting to get really nervous, a car driven by an elderly black man came out of nowhere and broadsided the truck—a diversionary tactic organized by the local NAACP to help the young couple escape.

The attraction between the young couple was clear, but unconsummated. Walker, influenced by broader forces within the black community that were skeptical of whites involved in the civil rights movement, was unsure of Leventhal's commitment to equality. Her fears were eased one night when they went swimming together with another volunteer, a white woman, and were discovered by the police. It would have been easy for Leventhal to blame the encounter on Walker, but he did not do so. As Walker noted, "Most white people in that situation would have automatically abandoned the black person. . . . Mel passed a major test that night because when he stood up to those state troopers and aligned himself with me, he showed courage" (White, 142). Soon they became romantically involved and she shared something very intimate with him: the manuscript to the still-unpublished *Once*. He noted, "I was smitten by Alice the first day I saw her, but I fell in love when I read *Once*" (White, 144). Although their relationship was unusual, it was not unique: Interracial romances were one predictable result of the civil rights movement, in which young, educated, principled men and women from across the country came together to work toward their lofty goal. Love just happened.

By the end of the summer, Walker and Leventhal were serious enough about each other that Walker was ready to take the next step: introducing him to her family. Her family liked him personally, but they were skeptical of his intentions toward her. In addition, Minnie Walker had never met a Jew, and did not have a good opinion of Jews in general. Her first comment to him was "You're one of those who killed Christ," to which he replied, "Well, Mrs. Walker, I don't think I was there at the time" (White, 148). Walker was mortified, but Leventhal took it in stride. Still it revealed some of the difficulties they would face over the course of their relationship. The visit only lasted a few days, but Walker's sister Ruth remembers being shocked when Alice told her that she was planning to marry Mel.

But Leventhal had one more year of law school to finish, so first he and Walker lived together in a small room near Washington Square Park in New York. It was in this tiny space that Walker began her first novel, *The Third Life of Grange Copeland*, about three generations of Georgia sharecroppers and their responses to the ingrained racism they faced. Leventhal taught Walker to swim and to drive a car. He supported her writing wholeheartedly, and was the first reader for much of her work. When she was awarded a writing residency at the prestigious MacDowell Colony in New Hampshire, he visited every weekend, but her weeks were free to complete the novel.

By March 1967, with the novel progressing nicely and Leventhal's graduation looming, Walker and Leventhal were married in a civil ceremony in New York City. Leventhal intended to return to Mississippi as a fully qualified lawyer, and Walker was determined to go with him. But in 1967 interracial marriage was still illegal in many parts of the South, including Mississippi, a struggle they would face together.

Mississippi

When the newlyweds returned to Mississippi in the summer of 1967, it was to a solid middle-class existence in a nice neighborhood. The Leventhals (Walker has always written under her birth name, but while she was married to Leventhal, she took his surname) were a nice young couple, despite the fact that their racial difference and political activism placed them outside both the law and the dominant culture in Mississippi. Leventhal went to work fighting school segregation and Walker returned to her novel. Leventhal was rapidly becoming well known as a civil rights attorney, a position of which he was proud, but which exposed the family to some risk from the same forces that had threatened them at the beginning of their relationship. In response they kept a loaded gun in the house, as well as a dog to protect them. It was a risky and stress-filled existence.

Meanwhile, Walker received two pieces of good news: An essay she had written in a single sitting, "The Civil Rights Movement: What Good Was It?", won an award and publication in a prestigious journal, *The American Scholar*. Even more exciting, her volume of poems, *Once*, had been accepted for publication. With work on the novel proceeding well, and recognition for both her poetry and nonfiction work, Walker was rapidly becoming well-known and well-regarded in her field.

At the same time, she went to work for the federal early-education program Head Start, a preschool program designed to give underprivileged children some preparation so that they might start school on a level playing field with their wealthier colleagues. Walker was charged with developing a curriculum to teach black Head Start teachers their own history, a history they could then share with their overwhelmingly black students. Walker was struck by the level of ignorance among the teachers and realized that, for many American blacks, the experiences of their own people were completely foreign to them. She developed an autobiography project, asking these women to tell their own stories, to help unlock the folk history of her people.

By spring 1968, Walker was pregnant again, this time joyfully. But on April 4, 1968, Martin Luther King Jr. was assassinated in Memphis, and soon after, Walker had a miscarriage. Numbed by tragedy, Walker recalls, "I did not even care. It seemed to me, at that time, that if 'he' (it was weeks before my tongue could form his name) must die, no one deserved to live, not even my own child" (White, 165). Walker and Leventhal marched in King's funeral cortege, an event she would later memorialize in her novel *Meridian*.

The year 1968 did not get better. Robert Kennedy, running for the Democratic nomination for president, was assassinated on the night of the California primary in June, and the Democratic National Convention in Chicago in August descended into riots and chaos. But Walker continued to write her harrowing novel and to collect accolades for *Once*.

Through 1969, she struggled with the book. She also became a professor when she was invited to fill in for Margaret Walker at Jackson State University. Though Jackson State was a historically black college, Margaret and then Alice Walker taught the only black literature classes. For Alice, the course was a rude awakening to the rifts forming in black culture, which dismissed the soaring rhetoric of the previous generation—including Langston Hughes (a personal friend of Walker, and the first to publish her work), Ernest Gaines, and Margaret Walker herself—as "old-timey" and "square" (White, 175).

In the late 1960s, black students were increasingly militant, recognizing the accomplishment of Martin Luther King Jr., but also the fact that even his moderate calls for basic justice had gotten him killed. This militancy crossed lines, having both political and artistic implications. On the artistic side, these students followed the lead of Richard Wright, who said that much early black writing "entered the court of American public opinion dressed in the knee pants of servility, curtsying to show that the Negro was not inferior." Instead these students were more drawn to the black arts movement. "Framed philosophically as 'the new black aesthetic,' the literary outpourings of these emerging writers would come to be known as the Black Arts movement, with 'death to whitey' one of the signature themes of their poems, stories, and plays" (White, 176). Walker, only in her mid-twenties, was closer in age to her students than the authors she was trying to introduce to them. But her sense of the black literary tradition was broader than the immediate concerns of the moment: She saw a width and scope that honored the work of black writers without consigning them to the Dumpster of history.

The year 1969 was also important for Walker because she gave birth to her daughter Rebecca that November. She completed *The Third Life of Grange Copeland* just days before she went into labor. Rebecca was a big, healthy baby of nearly ten pounds. Walker and Leventhal could not have been more pleased, though of course their relationship continued to raise the eyebrows and ire of strangers. Rebecca Walker, in her autobiography *Black, White and Jewish*, notes that one of her earliest memories is of her father sitting on their porch with a shotgun to ward off unfriendly visitors.

But for Alice, writing as a young mother was different from writing as a single woman or a member of a couple. Walker was simultaneously awed by the responsibility she now carried and frustrated at the conditions under which she lived. Leventhal traveled more and more, attempting

MEL LEVENTHAL AND ALICE WALKER HOLD THEIR BABY DAUGHTER, REBECCA. WALKER COMPLETED WORK ON HER FIRST NOVEL JUST DAYS BEFORE SHE WENT INTO LABOR.

to force school districts to respect the now fifteen-year-old Supreme Court decision *Brown* v. *Board of Education*, which called for the desegregation of schools, and spending many late nights at the NAACP office. Walker, then, was alone with an infant, her writing, and the continued threats of the Ku Klux Klan, a white supremacist group that burned crosses on the lawns of black and white supporters of civil rights and even killed people, and those who supported the KKK's tactics. Although the Leventhals had many friends in Jackson, they tended to be political rather than artistic friends, and Walker began to feel isolated, particularly as a writer.

The publication of *The Third Life of Grange Copeland* in 1970 marked Walker's arrival as a major American writer. The novel was critically acclaimed, but was also attacked for its portrayal of black men, particularly the blighted soul of Brownfield Copeland. Such responses would become a pattern for Walker: While the literary merit of her work was recognized, she would be attacked for placing her sympathies primarily with black women as victims of both white culture and, more immediately and personally (and, thus, more often), of black men. Walker began to get more press, and to be recognized by other writers. From being largely isolated in Jackson, she became a person people sought out, even in remote Mississippi.

But Mississippi was beginning to get to her. Living under an extended period of stress can often have serious psychological ramifications, and the violence always under the surface of the Leventhals' life in Mississippi was bound to take its toll. In addition, the dullness of small-town life was becoming a problem. As Mel Leventhal observed later, "She [Walker] felt stifled because we were living in a barren, cultureless, unsophisticated part of the country. I don't think she would have felt any different had she been married to a black man. . . . Alice loved the land and natural beauty of the South, but she could not abide the backwoods mentality and the lack of intellectual stimulation" (White, 209). To counteract this, she applied for and received a fellowship at Radcliffe University in Cambridge, Massachusetts.

In the summer of 1971, before she left for Radcliffe, Walker visited California by herself. Her old roommate, Diana Young, was living on a commune near San Francisco, and her old friend Robert Allen was located in that area as well. Walker loved the landscape of the Bay

Area, and was pleased to see her old friends, but she was filled with anxiety: Because of circumstances, she and Leventhal were planning to live apart, however temporarily, after only five years of marriage, and young Rebecca was coming to Cambridge with her mother.

Unfortunately the Radcliffe fellowship did not give Walker a lot of time to write. Both Walker and her daughter came down with a terrible flu that sidelined them for much of the winter, though Walker managed to design and teach a course at Wellesley College—then a woman's college—on black women writers. At the end of the year, with the novel which would become *Meridian* still in its infancy, Walker made two requests, one for herself, and one for her daughter. For herself, she asked for her Radcliffe residency to be extended another year, this time without pay. For her daughter, she asked that her father in Mississippi rescue her from the punishing climate that had made her so ill. These choices represented important crossroads in Walker's life. She also decided to leave her agent, Monica McCall, who had been her last link with Muriel Rukeyser. These decisions meant that, for Walker, her art was more important than her personal connections: understandable from the artist's perspective, but not necessarily from that of the spouse, or the child, or the mentor.

Walker's new agent, Wendy Weil, immediately placed Walker's story "Roselily" in a new magazine called *Ms.*, at this time just an insert in a weekly general interest publication called *New York* magazine. *Ms.*, the magazine at the forefront of the women's movement of the 1960s, and run by feminist celebrities such as Gloria Steinem, would be very influential for Walker during the next decade. She also began publishing her short fiction.

By the end of her time at Radcliffe in 1973, two dramatic events had occurred in Walker's life. Her beloved father Willie Lee had died; Walker would later pen a book of poetry and a novel in his memory. She had also committed herself to restoring the reputation of Zora Neale Hurston, a black woman writer from Florida whose 1937 masterpiece, *Their Eyes Were Watching God*, failed to save her from an unmarked pauper's grave. In 1973 Walker located Hurston's burial site and placed a simple headstone on the unnamed grave. These two powerful events spoke to both Walker's connection to the past, and her commitment to keeping it alive through her work.

She and Leventhal were also committed to giving their marriage one more chance, but not in Mississippi, to which Alice flatly refused to return. In the summer of 1973, they moved to New York, Leventhal to continue his work with the NAACP, and Walker to work as an associate editor at *Ms.* magazine. She was allowed a flexible work schedule that left time for her writing.

In 1974 Walker's book of poems, *Revolutionary Petunias*, was nominated for a National Book Award. Among the other poets nominated were Audre Lorde and Adrienne Rich. But Walker, Lorde, and Rich had promised one another something: If any of them won, they would accept the award on behalf of all of them and donate the stipend to a good cause. Adrienne Rich was announced as a co-winner with Allen Ginsburg, and as promised, she used her acceptance speech to explain how she was accepting the award on behalf of the three of them, and all women:

We together accept this award in the name of all women whose voices have gone and still go unheard in a patriarchal world, and in the name of those who, like us, have been tolerated as token women in this culture. . . . We believe that we can enrich ourselves more in supporting and giving to each other than in competing with each other; and that poetry—if it *is* poetry—exists in a realm beyond ranking and comparison. (White, 271)

Feminism in the 1970s was filled, if not with this same sense of self-denying sisterhood, then at least with a sense that women could choose to structure their lives, their families, and their careers differently. Of course, such restructurings came at some cost, and Walker in particular has been the subject of some very cutting remarks by her now-estranged daughter Rebecca, who saw in Walker's attempts to refocus their relationship her mother's abandonment and lack of concern.

Yet it was not Rebecca that Walker left, ultimately. It was Mel Leventhal. Despite moving to New York, the tensions in their marriage caused by Mississippi remained, unable to restore the early bonds that had seen them through so many crises in the early days of their relationship. Walker simply felt, she said, unsuited for marriage. She and Rebecca moved to a small apartment in another part of Brooklyn in 1976, and Walker and Leventhal filed for an amicable, if sad, divorce. The parents agreed that, for the sake of stability, they would share custody in two-year terms, with Walker taking the first turn.

It was during this time that Walker reestablished her connection with Robert Allen, her old friend from Atlanta and California, whose interest in her was clear. He was the editor of a journal called *The Black Scholar*, based in California, and had what was known then as an "open" marriage, meaning that neither partner expected sexual fidelity from the other. Thus Allen was free to have a relationship with Walker, although she was not free to have one with him. But when Allen was in New York to interview Alex Haley about his bestselling novel *Roots*, Walker told him of her separation and they became involved soon after. Mel Leventhal married again, this time to Judith Goldsmith, whom he had dated before their marriage, soon after the divorce. Goldsmith was very much a traditional wife, and much of Rebecca Walker's writing about her parents draws upon the distinction between the homemaker Goldsmith and the disengaged professional Walker as models of parenting.

Also in 1976, Walker completed and published the novel that examined closely the field upon which she and Leventhal had met: the civil rights movement. *Meridian* is a taut, though nonchronological, narrative of the journey of a young woman into and out of the movement, and involves extended considerations of the issues surrounding interracial relationships, the right role of violence in addressing social wrongs, and the mystical power of nature.

Although Walker was fond of Allen, he was still married. It was this, as much as anything else, that kept Walker tied to the East Coast. In addition to her work at *Ms.*, she was also helping unknown women writers get published at *Ms.* and in other publications. And she was writing, primarily poetry. But in 1978, when Rebecca went to live with her father and Allen separated from his wife, she moved west.

California

In the novel that was taking shape in her head, according to her biographer Evelyn White, "the characters (Southern, full of spunk) . . . had made clear their displeasure with screeching subways and towering skyscrapers that, to their mind, seemed to block God's view" (310). Clearly this was to be a "country" book, and would require a rural setting. Walker and Allen settled on Boonville, a small village in Northern California so isolated it had its own dialect. She continued to work for *Ms.* long-distance, and lived off a fellowship from the Guggenheim Foundation while she crafted the novel that would become *The Color Purple*.

But as always, controversy followed Walker. In 1979 she became unintentionally embroiled in a debate over a book by Michele Wallace, *Black Macho and the Myth of the Superwoman*, which examined the contentious relations between black men and women. Wallace argued that black men had insisted that black women submerge their gender identity during the civil rights era in the interest of broader racial solidarity, and that for many black men, white women were a sign of success: That is, black women were intended to be left behind by successful black men.

As with other works by black women that laid the cause of their problems in greater or lesser degrees at the feet of black men, the book was loudly and swiftly criticized. But *Ms.*, the preeminent feminist journal of the day, featured excerpts and gave *Black Macho* a cover story. Walker, who was seen by many in the black community as the representative of black interests at *Ms.*, was blamed for this public airing of an "inside" matter, and came in for her share of criticism, though she had nothing to do with the article. Walker's longtime acquaintance, poet June Jordan, panned the book in the *New York Times*. It did not help that much of the black male response to the book was featured in *The Black Scholar*, edited by Walker's boyfriend, Robert Allen.

Walker insisted as always on the right of black women to tell the truth the way that they saw it. And in any case, she was deeply involved in her writing of a book that would, in short order, come in for many of the same criticisms as Wallace's, though *The Color Purple* held out a chance for redemption for both black men and women, a redemption based on embracing sexuality, nature, respect, and equality.

She was also publishing prolifically: a book of poems dedicated to her father, *Good Night Willie Lee, I'll See You in the Morning*, and an anthology of the work of Zora Neale Hurston, *I Love Myself When I Am Laughing . . . And Then Again When I Am Looking Mean and Impressive.* In short order, these were followed by the collection of short stories *You Can't Keep a Good Woman Down.* When one considers that all this was going on as she was writing *The Color Purple,* the achievement is more impressive and speaks to the creative fervor that California unleashed.

The Color Purple

Even in manuscript form, readers of the novel realized that they had something important in their hands. Barbara Smith, a student of Walker's at Wellesley and author of the important 1977 essay "Toward a Black Feminist Criticism," called the novel "radically brilliant," and Walker's boss at *Ms.,* Gloria Steinem, wrote "It is wonderful—I mean, full of wonder." Gossip in the publishing industry was that "Alice Walker [had] delivered a 'big book'" (White, 341). *Ms.* released a special fiction issue in June 1982 with Walker on the cover, declaring her "A Major American Author." This cover photo precipitated a crisis in Walker's self-image that she discusses in her essay "Beauty: When the Other Dancer Is the Self."

This much was clear: *The Color Purple* was destined to change Walker's life forever. For one thing, she was now very much a figure in the public eye. This only became more dramatic when, in 1983, she became the first black woman to be awarded a Pulitzer Prize for fiction. That designation was hardly a given, however: The chair of the jury was a noted conservative and antifeminist author, Midge Decter, unlikely to be sympathetic to the story of a poor abused black girl who finds her way back to God through homosexuality. And indeed, Decter fought hard to prevent the book from even being considered. But the other two jurors, Peter S. Prescott and John Clellon Holmes, believed so strongly in the novel that they overcame Decter's arguments. Prescott later noted that

THE COLOR PURPLE WAS A SMASH. IT BECAME A BEST-SELLING, AWARD-WINNING NOVEL, AND A MOVIE THAT LAUNCHED OR ENRICHED CAREERS. FINALLY, IT BECAME A PLAY PRODUCED BY OPRAH WINFREY, WHO STANDS ON STAGE WITH ALICE WALKER (*LEFT*) ON OPENING NIGHT.

The Color Purple was as much a cultural event as a novel:

> Over time, *The Color Purple* has achieved a status
> that few books ever attain. It is one of the few
> books that is read by most students in the country.
> It has become a rite of passage.
>
> It is also one of the few literary books to capture
> the popular imagination and leave a permanent
> imprint on our society. There are some commer-
> cial books that did that, like *The Godfather* and
> *Jaws*. But *The Color Purple* is literature of the
> highest form. (White, 356–357).

A recipient of the National Book Award and a *New
York Times* best-seller, the novel established Walker as a
household name.

More importantly, it gave Walker the economic freedom so important to creative endeavors. Walker understood that money allowed artists to pursue their goals.
Virginia Woolf is remembered for insisting that women
artists needed "A Room of One's Own" to create, but it is
often forgotten that she insisted just as strongly on an
independent income as a precondition for creative freedom. Walker understood this necessity too. She had
mourned for Zora Neale Hurston, saying:

> Financial dependency is the thread that sewed a
> cloud over Hurston's life, from the time she left
> home to work as a maid at fourteen to the day of
> her death. It is ironic that this woman, who many
> claimed sold her soul to record the sources of
> authentic, black American folk art (whereas it is
> apparently cool to sell your soul for a university
> job, say, or a new car) and who was made of some
> of the universe's most naturally free stuff . . . was
> denied even a steady pittance, free from strings,

that would have kept her secure enough to do her best work. . . . Only after she died penniless . . . still following her vision and her road, did it begin to seem to some that yes, perhaps this woman was a serious artist after all. But you're up against a hard game if you have to die to win it, and we must insist that dying in poverty is an unacceptable extreme.

The success of *The Color Purple*, then, freed Walker from those constraints, and has allowed her the freedom for more than twenty-five years to live as she pleases.

Such freedom did not come without controversy, however. *The Color Purple* awoke all the same protests that had plagued Ntozake Shange when *For Colored Girls Who Have Considered Suicide When the Rainbow is Enuf* and Michele Wallace after the publication of *Black Macho*. And because the book was so groundbreaking and so successful, the controversy exploded beyond the black community. When the book was made into a mainstream film by Steven Spielberg, the controversy intensified.

Yet again, Walker's work was discussed only in terms of its representation of black men, with no real indication that she had provided, within the novel itself, a road map for healthy relationships between black men and women. Instead she faced protests so stringent and unyielding that she gave up many public appearances, including a chance to introduce James Baldwin, one of her idols and the author of the classic novel *Go Tell it on the Mountain*. Walker's success had other drawbacks as well. With increased visibility came increased demands on her time. Robert Allen confessed that he had been unfaithful to her, and her daughter, Rebecca, was openly critical of her mother's busy travel and appearance schedule. In her 2000 autobiography, *Black, White, and Jewish*, Rebecca

REBECCA WALKER PUBLISHED A MEMOIR HIGHLY CRITICAL OF HER FAMOUS MOTHER.

Leventhal Walker (as she legally changed her name in 1986) describes her mother as self-absorbed and inattentive to her needs. Rebecca became sexually active at a young age, with her mother's knowledge, and by fourteen had requested her mother's help to get an abortion. Despite the criticisms she leveled at both her parents in the book, she ended fundamentally ambivalent. But in 2004, when Rebecca announced to her mother that she was expecting a child, Walker received the news coldly. What followed was a flurry of letters between the two women, culminating with Alice Walker reportedly saying that "our relationship had been inconsequential for years" and that "she was no longer interested in being [Rebecca's] mother. She even signed the letter with her first name, rather than 'Mom'." Rebecca Walker published a book in 2008, *Baby Love: Choosing Motherhood after a Lifetime of Ambivalence*, which addresses many of these issues and chronicles her relationship with her son Tenzin, whom Alice Walker has never seen.

Walker, settled happily in California, used some of the proceeds from the novel to start her own publishing house, Wild Trees Press (active 1984–1988), and build her own home in the mountains. She revealed her bisexuality after the release of *The Color Purple* and had a long affair with folk-pop singer Tracy Chapman.

None of her later works had the same critical and commercial success as *The Color Purple*, but as Walker herself noted in her 1988 book *Living By the Word*, "In some ways, I feel my early life's work is done, and done completely. The books I have produced already carry forward the thoughts that I feel the ancestors were trying to help me pass on."

Walker continues to write. Many of her more recent works are concerned with large-scale issues such as female genital mutilation or sweeping concerns such as reincarnation and the nature of the goddess. She is also openly political. In the wake of the September 11, 2001, attacks on the United States, she wrote *Sent by Earth: A Message from the Grandmother Spirit After the Attacks on the World Trade Center and the Pentagon*, which asks the question "Where do we start? How do we reclaim a proper relationship with the world?" and attempts to contextualize the attacks as a response to the larger context of American aggression, both to foreign nations and to its own internal minorities.

In the end, Walker's life and enormous body of work stick closely to her concerns with women, people of color, and justice. Her defense of the environment, opposition to globalization, and interest in alternative forms of knowledge are consistent with this worldview.

ACTORS WEARING KU KLUX KLAN GARB RIDE ON HORSES AT NIGHT IN A STILL FROM THE FAMOUS—AND INFAMOUS—FILM, *BIRTH OF A NATION*.

Chapter 2

Walker and Her Times

As one of the most prominent voices in black women's literature, Alice Walker brings a wide array of historical and cultural information to her work, not all of which may be equally familiar to contemporary readers. She pulls her material from both individual and communal sources, though as someone who lived through some of the most turbulent times in recent American history, there's a blurry line between her own experiences and those of the broader society. Born into the Jim Crow–era South, active in the civil rights and feminist movements, and determined to share the history of her people, particularly the accomplishments of black women, with others, she integrates a great deal of cultural context into her deeply spiritual and personal writing.

Jim Crow Era

The profoundly inhumane institution of slavery was an important aspect of American economic and social life almost since European settlers began coming to North America in the seventeenth century. In 1863, during the American Civil War (1861–1865), President Abraham Lincoln signed the Emancipation Proclamation, ending slavery. But in the years following the war, many of the former slaveholding states put into place a series of laws designed to keep blacks and whites separated in most areas of civic, social, and economic life, including education, transportation, and even bathrooms, with whites getting preferential treatment in every case.

These laws were known as Jim Crow laws. The name came from a song called "Jump Jim Crow," reputedly written about a lame black performer in Cincinnati, but performed by a white in blackface in a "minstrel show," a common form of stage entertainment that reveals the depth of casual racism that was rampant in nineteenth-century American culture. Minstrel show performers generally wore coal-black makeup, with wide, caricatured red-and-white mouths. This song, written and performed by T. D. "Daddy" Rice, was somewhat unusual in that it asserted: "Should dey get to fighting/ Perhaps de blacks will rise/ For deir wish for freedon / Is shining in deir eyes." Nevertheless, the mode of performance, and the minstrel movement generally, strengthened racist perceptions of African Americans as slow, lazy, and subhuman.

What minstrel shows established in the public consciousness, Jim Crow laws established in public policy. It is true that, after emancipation, blacks generally gravitated to their own communities, churches, and schools. However, there is a great difference between forming a community and being prevented by law from participating in public life. In a series of laws passed generally between 1890 and 1910 (and confirmed by the Supreme Court decision *Plessy* v. *Ferguson*, 1896), pervasive discrimination became the law. "Most of these legal steps were aimed at separating the races in public spaces (public schools, parks, accommodations, and transportation) and preventing adult black males from exercising the right to vote. In every state of the former Confederacy, the system of legalized segregation and disfranchisement was fully in place by 1910" ("History of Jim Crow"). This was the era of *Birth of a Nation* (1915), the famously racist film by D. W. Griffith, the father of modern cinema. It was based on the novel *The Clansman*, by Thomas Dixon. Both Dixon and Griffith were southerners. D. W. Griffith, and possibly Dixon, were sons of Confederate soldiers. In addition, Dixon had been the college roommate of Woodrow Wilson, who was president at the time the film was released.

Under Jim Crow laws, black Americans were relegated to separate but never really equal facilities. Keeping races separate in public spaces such as train stations required two of everything: two waiting rooms, two drinking fountains, two bathrooms. As one Southern white who was critical of Jim Crow noted, "White people were so fixated on maintaining two of everything, that we didn't have one good anything. The result has been an affliction of ignorance, mediocrity and backwardness that is still crippling the South today" (White, 10). Of course this long-term humiliation of people being told that they are not even good enough to sit next to had to have a profound effect on those living with this system, but its most far-reaching effects may have been in the field of education. Walker herself attended segregated schools throughout her time in school, including one located in a former prison. Such substandard facilities made it very difficult to get a solid education, even for a student as motivated as Walker.

Many blacks, including Walker's older siblings, had little patience with life under these conditions. They participated in a massive wave of migration from the Deep South to the cities of the North: New York, Boston, Chicago, Detroit. There, although they may have only been able to work in factories, with limited opportunity for advancement, at least they could eat where they liked and ride the bus to work with some dignity. And their salaries were their own to spend, unlike the sharecropping economy of the Deep South, where part of every crop went to the landlord. Walker's siblings and others who moved north in search of opportunity could reasonably expect to do better than their fathers had done.

The beginning of the end of the Jim Crow era happened on December 1, 1955, when a woman named Rosa Parks refused to give up her seat on a Montgomery, Alabama, bus to a white passenger. Though transportation companies generally did not run two separate buses, they did enforce distinct seating areas within a single vehicle, with blacks riding in the back. Parks, a local secretary for the NAACP as well as a seamstress, resisted the simple but humiliating request to move, and so became a heroine of the civil rights movement. Over the next decade, appeals for racial justice grew increasingly forceful, culminating in the Civil Rights Act of 1964.

The Civil Rights Movement

African Americans may have been freed by the Emancipation Proclamation, but their white neighbors were not often interested in granting them any meaningful change in status, as we have seen. For ninety years, segregation was the rule, even when it was not the law. The Supreme Court decision *Brown* v. *Board of Education* (1954) officially ended segregation in education, though many states were slow to comply. Actual implementation required many courageous acts by the individuals who participated in what would come to be known as the civil rights movement.

The National Association for the Advancement of Colored People (NAACP) had been founded in 1909 by W. E. B. DuBois and others, but was reinvigorated by the civil rights movement. Their first major action was the Montgomery Bus Boycott, which began in late 1955, after the arrest of Parks. For months African Americans, as well as Caucasians who agreed with their goals, rode bicycles, carpooled, and walked to work in a boycott of the system that relegated blacks to second-class citizenship. White citizens who supported segregation responded by instituting minimum taxi fares, trying to get insurance policies on black drivers cancelled, and even firebombing the homes of two black ministers: Reverend Ralph Abernathy, and a new national figure, Reverend Martin Luther King Jr. A June decision in federal district court and a November decision by the Supreme Court (*Browder* v. *Gayle*, 1956) finally struck down the segregation of public transportation in Alabama and other states.

With Martin Luther King Jr.'s founding of the Southern Christian Leadership Conference (SCLC) in 1957, and the establishment of the Student Nonviolent Coordinating Committee (SNCC) in 1960, already ongoing protests at segregated lunch counters were given some structure: planned and coordinated rather than spontaneous individual acts. King, the first president of the SCLC, helped formulate general principles for the movement, including nonviolence and civil disobedience. King insisted that, in their quest for justice, civil rights activists could not become like the racist forces they opposed, urging: "We must forever conduct our struggle on the high plane of dignity and discipline" (Brunner & Haney). King was following the lead of the Indian leader Mohandas K. "Mahatma" Gandhi, who had articulated his own theory of nonviolent resistance as a response to the repression of the British Empire in his native land. King adapted Gandhi's principles with great success, and through a combination of individual and organized action, the civil rights movement contested segregation in many areas of public life.

The civil rights workers often faced stiff opposition, including the resistance or active intervention of state and local law enforcement against them. Students frequently were forced to integrate schools throughout the South under the protection of federal troops, since local law enforcement refused to protect them. In one landmark case, as many as 5,000 troops were needed to ensure the safety of James Meredith when he began his studies at the University of Mississippi. The Freedom Riders, an integrated group organized by the Chicago-based organization Congress for Racial Equality (CORE), were routinely beaten when blacks and whites rode together on interstate bus lines through the South. Some particularly resistant officials, such as the Birmingham, Alabama, commissioner of public safety "Bull" Connor, used high-pressure fire hoses and attack dogs on peaceful protesters, injuring many, including schoolchildren ("Project 'C' in Birmingham").

Meanwhile, black consciousness was also being raised in urban areas across the country by the Nation of Islam. Founded in 1930 in Detroit, the Nation of Islam used the

"BULL" CONNOR, THE RACIST COMMISSIONER OF PUBLIC SAFETY IN BIRMINGHAM, ALABAMA, DIRECTED FIREFIGHTERS TO TURN THEIR HOSES ON PEACEFUL CIVIL RIGHTS DEMONSTRATORS.

teachings of the Prophet Muhammad to voice a very specific religious vision privileging the experiences of black Americans—that blacks were the original humans, that whites represent Satan, and that American slavery was prophesied in the Bible. None of these beliefs corresponds to those of mainstream Islam, which judges people by their behavior, not their race. Faithful Muslims consider followers of the Nation of Islam heretics. In addition, the Nation of Islam centered a tremendous amount of power in its founder, W. D. Fard, and his chief disciple and eventual replacement, Elijah Muhammad, who led the organization from 1935 until his death in 1975.

Members of the Nation of Islam were notable partly because of the strictly disciplined and regulated way they conducted themselves: The Nation of Islam prescribed what their members ate, their bathing rituals, and what they wore. Most white Americans became aware of the Nation of Islam through the ascendency of Malcolm X as a civil rights leader. An impassioned and intelligent man, Malcolm X made an eloquent case for the systemic racism of American culture and the necessity for blacks to resist "by any means necessary." He was assassinated in 1965, probably because he had shifted from Nation of Islam beliefs to those of mainstream Islam and had even become a *hajji*, that is, someone who made the pilgrimage to Mecca in Saudi Arabia, Islam's holiest site. This transition to the larger world of Islam alienated him from his own movement and caused his mentor, Elijah Muhammad, to view him as a traitor. But he remained until his death—and after it, symbolically—an important representative of what came to be known Black Nationalism.

Other major events of the era include the March on Washington in 1963. At the march, Martin Luther King Jr. delivered his momentous "I Have a Dream" speech. In it he argued not for the racial supremacy of blacks, as the Nation of Islam did, but rather for genuine equality.

> I have a dream that one day this nation will rise up
> and live out the true meaning of its creed: "We
> hold these truths to be self-evident, that all men
> are created equal." . . . I have a dream that my
> four little children will one day live in a nation
> where they will not be judged by the color of their
> skin, but by the content of their character. . . . I
> have a dream that one day on the red hills of
> Georgia the sons of former slaves and the sons of
> former slave owners will be able to sit down
> together at a table of brotherhood.

The huge upswell of these and other mass demonstra-
tions culminated in the Civil Rights Act of 1964, which
banned most forms of legal segregation.

Several barriers to full equality remained, however.
One of these was voter registration, from which blacks
were often barred by poverty and literacy requirements, as
well as openly menaced by some local racists. It was to
correct this injustice that Alice Walker went to Mississippi
to register voters. Instead of doing so, however, she was
put to work collecting depositions from people who had
been evicted from their homes when they registered to
vote. Such evidence would be used to challenge
Mississippi's contention that it was in compliance with the
Voting Rights Act of 1965. There she worked with Mel
Leventhal, a lawyer from New York, and faced harassment
and threats at every turn, though her behavior was per-
fectly legal.

But Walker's developing relationship with Leventhal
ran afoul of the last major barrier to equality: a series of
laws in several states banning the practice they called
"miscegenation"—that is, racial mixing through marriage. In 1958 Richard and Mildred Loving, residents of
Virginia, were married in nearby Washington, D.C. He
was a white man and she was a black woman. When they

AS THE 1960S WORE ON, THOSE SEEKING EQUAL RIGHTS BECAME MORE MILITANT. MALCOLM X, A LEADER OF THE BLACK MUSLIMS, WHO BELIEVED IN RACIAL SEPARATISM, HERE ATTENDS A TRIAL OF FOURTEEN BLACK MUSLIMS. HE IS ATTENDED BY VEILED BLACK MUSLIM WOMEN.

returned to Virginia, they were tried for the crime of miscegenation, illegal in their home state, and sentenced to one year in prison each, with the sentence to be suspended on the condition that they left the state. They did so, but contacted the American Civil Liberties Union (ACLU) to challenge the Virginia law. This controversial case went all the way to the Supreme Court, which decided, in *Loving v. Virginia* (1967), that laws banning interracial marriage were unconstitutional. Several states continued to resist with Alabama being the last to strike down their law in 2000 ("Alabama Removes Ban").

IN THE 1960S (AND, IN SOME STATES, STILL LATER), RACIAL INTERMAR-
RIAGE WAS ILLEGAL. RICHARD AND MILDRED LOVING WERE ARRESTED
WHEN THEY TRIED TO LIVE TOGETHER AS A MARRIED COUPLE IN THEIR
NATIVE STATE OF VIRGINIA. THEY TOOK THEIR CASE ALL THE WAY TO
THE SUPREME COURT, WHICH RULED IN THEIR FAVOR IN 1967.

Even after the successes of 1964, 1965, and 1968, tensions remained within the black community, often mirroring those in the broader political field. Young people across the nation in the late 1960s and early 1970s were frustrated that the nonviolent tactics of their leaders had

had so little influence on the political changes they hoped to effect: The war dragged on, violence was increasingly a response to peaceful protests, and they found themselves dismissed by the dominant culture as "hippies": colorful and decadent, but not influential. For many, increasing militancy was the response. Some antiwar groups even turned to violence in their frustration.

Young blacks were not immune to this change in the environment. Separatist movements had appeared periodically in black culture: Marcus Garvey, for example, writing and speaking in the 1920s, thought blacks should repatriate to Africa. The racial classifications of the Nation of Islam insisted on concrete lines between blacks and whites as well. Out of this movement grew the Black Nationalist movement, which identified race as the first and most important aspect of identity, and thus stood against the integrationist tide of the broader civil rights movement. These tensions would have artistic consequences as well.

Music: The Blues and Jazz

An important aspect of Alice Walker's work, particularly *The Color Purple*, is the use of music, and specifically the blues. The blues are a distinctly American musical form, closely related to, and often blended with, jazz. Although the development of the blues, like most genres, is somewhat mysterious, most experts agree that the form was well established by 1910 or so, approximately the same period as the beginning of *The Color Purple*. It developed primarily in the South, in the communities of former slaves. Credit generally goes to bandleader W. C. Handy, whose 1912 song "Memphis Blues" represents one of the earliest uses of the term.

The blues were one of the first forms of nonreligious music in the African-American community, and they reflected an individual voice and consciousness quite unlike the spirituals from which they developed. According to one historian, "there was a direct relationship between the national ideological emphasis upon the individual, the popularity of Booker T. Washington's teachings, and the rise of the blues" (Levine, 223). That is, a new and rising sense of the importance of the individual in his or her own right led to this new form, in which personal experience was particularly important, leading to a focus on romantic pursuits rather than the comforts offered by God to the downtrodden. Lyrically many blues songs concentrated on the difficulties of personal relationships, particularly love problems with unappreciative or cheating partners. Even structurally, the blues emphasized this new "voice," generally following a call-and-response pattern between a single singer and a single guitarist.

Early on, these singers were often women. The era known as classic blues, basically the 1920s and 1930s, was dominated by female singers. Mamie Smith's 1920 hit "Crazy Blues" is an early example of this phenomenon, but figures such as Bessie Smith, Ma Rainey, Alberta Hunter, and Ethel Waters also had a major impact on the form.

One possible model for the character of Shug Avery in *The Color Purple* was Bessie Smith, one of the first blues superstars. Born in Chattanooga, Tennessee, in 1892, she was orphaned at a young age, and sang and danced on the streets to help her family make ends meet. By 1912 she was dancing with the Moses Stokes Minstrel Troupe, where her older brother was also employed, as was Ma Rainey. Eventually Smith got regular singing jobs in New York and Atlanta, and traveled the East and the South singing at various clubs. It was a difficult life, working at jobs that did not pay well. But she was refining her skills, and by 1923, she was making records. Smith prospered through the 1920s, touring with her own show. She performed in a tent, like a circus, so that she did not even need theaters, and she had her own railroad car. She married in 1923, but the marriage was not happy: She and her husband fought violently, and both partners were unfaithful. They did not live together after 1930.

Like a lot of performers, Smith was hit hard by the Great Depression. She continued to record and tour, but she was less popular than before. Her musical style was also changing, leaning more toward swing in her last recording sessions. Some mystery surrounds Smith's death: Undoubtedly, she was in a serious car accident in 1937, but questions surround her treatment. Legend has it that Smith was refused treatment at a whites-only hospital, and by the time she reached the black hospital, she had lost too much blood to be saved. Smith's biographer, Chris Albertson, has conclusively proven this story false: Both white and black ambulances appeared at the accident scene, and Smith was taken directly to the blacks-only hospital. In a 2003 interview, Albertson noted that the original story has proved tenacious, possibly because it is perceived as being more telling about the nature of life under Jim Crow.

Another prominent early blues singer is Gertrude "Ma" Rainey. She was born in 1886 in Georgia, and was performing in public by the age of fourteen. In 1902, while traveling with a vaudeville show, she heard a young woman in St. Louis singing a song that she adopted as her own. Rainey claimed to have coined the term *the blues* for the form, but there is no independent evidence of that. In 1904 she married William "Pa" Rainey, and together they toured as "Rainey & Rainey: Assassinators of the Blues."

Despite her marriage, Rainey had a taste for much younger men, and for women, suggesting that she, too, might be a model for Walker's Shug. In 1925 she was arrested at a party in Chicago in a room of scantily clad women. She also recorded the song "Prove It on Me Blues," in which she claimed: "I went out last night with a crowd of my friends, / It must've been women, 'cause I don't like no men. / Wear my clothes just like a fan/ Talk to the gals just like any old man." In *The Color Purple*, Celie thinks of Shug that "she talk and act sometimes like a man" (81). Although her usual stage persona was the standard passionate woman-done-wrong by a no-good man, on the cover of this record, she appears in a peculiar outfit: She is wearing a skirt, but above the waist, she is dressed as a man, in a suit coat and vest, tie, man's hat— a very unusual outfit for a woman at that time—and she's talking to two attractive young women, apparently flirting with them. All the women are laughing.

Rainey, who was known as the Mother of the Blues, performed for many years and recorded prolifically. Like Smith, she was hit hard by the Depression. But she had done well enough in her career that she could retire in 1933, and she returned to her native Georgia and opened two theaters. She died in 1939 of a heart attack.

The blues took on an increasingly political tone, as demonstrated by the moving and troubling 1939 song "Strange Fruit," a staple of Billie Holiday's repertoire, which addressed the problem of racially motivated vigilante "justice" known as lynching, in which black men were hung from trees for various transgressions, usually, though not always, involving white women.

Southern trees bear strange fruit,
Blood on the leaves and blood at the root,
Black bodies swinging in the southern breeze,
Strange fruit hanging from the poplar trees.

It's hard to overestimate the amount of controversy this song, based on a poem by Abel Meeropol, generated: Reportedly, Holiday was nervous about the subject matter when she first performed the song at the integrated nightclub Café Society in New York's Greenwich Village. She kept the song in her repertoire for more than twenty years because, she said, it reminded her of her father's death. But the song was frequently misunderstood, and in 1959, Holiday complained that people would request it by asking for "that sexy song about people swinging" (Smith). There was nothing sexy about lynching, still a very loaded topic: As recently as 2007, in Jena, Louisiana, nooses were hung from a reputed "whites-only" tree in front of the local high school, triggering a national debate on racism and the legacy of the Jim Crow era.

Like her predecessors, Billie Holiday also had great difficulties in her personal life, including multiple instances of rape and incarceration, drug abuse, and a stint as a prostitute in her teens. But by the age of eighteen or so, she was singing regularly in clubs around Harlem, and her emotional, textured voice was redefining jazz performance. Holiday saw her voice as an instrument and herself less a singer than an instrumentalist: "I don't think I'm singing. I feel like I am playing a horn. I try to improvise like Les Young, Louis Armstrong or someone else I admire. What comes out is what I feel. I hate straight singing. I have to change a tune to my own way of doing it. That's all I know" (Hentoff and Shapiro, 201). Her work was unusual, distinctive. As she aged, her voice became more fragile, but the music she recorded toward the end of her career was, if anything, more lush and rich than her early work.

A series of unhappy love affairs and a lifelong substance abuse problem took their toll, however. She began using hard drugs in the early 1940s. Although she married trombone player Jimmy Monroe in 1941, she soon left her husband to live with her drug dealer, trumpet player Joe Guy. Both relationships disintegrated around 1947, the same year she was jailed on drug charges in West Virginia and lost her New York City cabaret card, which was required in order to perform in venues serving alcohol, a staple of any performer's professional career. The latter of these calamities barred her from performing in her home city almost entirely in the last decade of her life, though she did appear in one film and on television, as well as in live concerts, both in the United States and in Europe. Her health was clearly failing. At a May 1959 benefit concert, she was able to sing only two songs, and less than a week later, she was hospitalized with heart and liver disease. She was placed under house arrest in the hospital when drugs were discovered in her possession, and she died in New York in July 1959.

The tragedies of the women of the blues era, however sad, demonstrate a particular kind of strength and tenaciousness that depends on an identity formed not through marriage, nor through religion, nor through traditional feminine values. These women were strong, they lived through tough times, and they took their suffering and turned it into art. Small wonder, then, that Alice Walker should see in these figures models for her own liberatory womanist project.

The Women's Movement and "Womanism"

Just as Walker had been involved in the civil rights movement in the 1960s, she also became a leading member of the women's movement in the 1970s, defining a particular brand of black feminism.

Women's rights had been a point of contention long before the twentieth-century women's movement. Mary Wollstonecraft had argued for women's rights as part of the broader liberation movements that produced the American and French revolutions in the late eighteenth century, and as the nineteenth century segued into the twentieth, women called "suffragettes" fought hard to earn the right to vote in elections. The modern American women's movement, however, was born out of the economics of World War II, when large numbers of women replaced men in factories across the United States. After the war, women were expected to return home, but many now chafed under the restraints of housekeeping and child-rearing, and longed to do more with their lives.

Popular discontent found a voice in 1963, when Betty Friedan published her groundbreaking work *The Feminine Mystique*. In it, Friedan argued that women faced "the problem that has no name"—that is, that even women who had achieved what they were taught to want were dissatisfied with their lives. Basing her research on an elite, white population (her classmates from the Smith College class of 1942), Friedan drew broad conclusions about the frustrations that women faced. The book, a best seller, ignited a storm of controversy and brought the fledgling women's movement into broader public consciousness. Friedan was also a cofounder of the

THE WOMEN'S RIGHTS MOVEMENT SPRANG UP ALONGSIDE THE PUSH FOR CIVIL RIGHTS. WHEN GLORIA STEINEM AND PATRICIA CARBINE (*RIGHT*) FOUNDED THE FEMINIST MAGAZINE *MS.*, THEY FOUND AN ADVOCATE AND CONTRIBUTOR IN ALICE WALKER.

National Organization of Women (NOW), and its first president.

Another prominent figure in the women's movement was reporter and political activist Gloria Steinem. Originally writing in male magazines such as *Esquire*, Steinem cofounded the first mainstream magazine dedicated to feminist issues, *Ms.*, in 1972. The name of the magazine sought to avoid the usual titles for women, Miss and Mrs., both of which mark a woman's relationship status, unlike the neutral Mister. In the 1970s, *Ms.* published stories about abortion, domestic abuse, sex-trafficking, and gender inequity, all issues of particular interest to women. Steinem was an early and avid supporter of Alice Walker's work, offering her a flexible position at the magazine in 1974, and for many years thereafter.

Walker and Steinem became friends while working together. Walker resisted, however, the term *feminist*, because she thought it ignored the particular problems of women of color. Instead, she preferred the term *womanist*, which she coined to describe those experiences. She defined the term in the preface to her 1983 essay collection, *In Search of Our Mother's Gardens*:

> **Womanist** 1. From womanish. (Opp of "girlish," i.e. frivolous, irresponsible, not serious.) A black feminist or feminist of color. From the black folk expression of mothers to female children, "You acting womanish," i.e. like a woman. Usually referring to outrageous, audacious, courageous or *willful* behavior. (xi, original emphasis)
> Womanist is to feminist as purple is to lavender. (xii)

Womanism, then, allowed Walker to define a particular aspect of the women's movement as it applied to her own experience and those of others like her.

Black Women Writers (The Sisterhood)

In the 1970s and 1980s, writing by American women of color exploded, partly as a result of self-conscious acts on the part of the writers themselves, and partly because a generation of educated black women with expanded opportunities for publication all matured more or less simultaneously. These women were raised on the forces of the civil rights movement, the black arts movement (which sought to define a particular African-American aesthetic in literature and other arts), the women's movement, the gay rights movement, the sexual liberation movement, the antiwar movement, and the various countercultural communities that sprang up in those exciting, if troubled, times. These liberation movements combined to empower and authorize voices that had largely been suppressed at other times in history, and the women involved were determined to help one another publish, and to affirm the value of each other's voices.

During the 1970s, for example, a group of black women artists in New York were loosely gathered as a group called simply "The Sisterhood." They met in the Brooklyn apartment of poet and activist June Jordan (1936–2002), a first-generation American of Jamaican descent. Walker was a regular at these gatherings, as was Ntozake Shange, whose play *For Colored Girls Who Have Considered Suicide When the Rainbow Is Enuf* had been produced to great accolades in 1975, but who was undergoing a fierce critique from some members of the black community because of the representation of black men in the play (thus prefiguring Walker's own difficulties with similar issues to come). Part reading group, part consciousness-raising group, part political discussion, The Sisterhood provided support of every kind to creative women who were struggling with the multiple concerns of racism, sexism, family, and art. Other members of the immediate and extended circle included Gloria Naylor,

Toni Morrison, Toni Cade Bambara, Barbara Smith, Audre Lorde, and Nikki Giovanni.

But even outside their circle, things were happening to change the face of American literature. Coming out of the black arts movement Giovanni and Shange brought an explicitly politicized sense of racial identity to their work. Founded by Amiri Baraka (born LeRoi Jones), the black arts movement was a model for reclaiming one's cultural voice in the face of an often heedless majority population. It was influential, inspiring many other ethnic literature and arts movements. As Ishmael Reed noted, "there would be no multiculturalism movement without Black Arts. Latinos, Asian Americans, and others all say they began writing as a result of the example of the 1960s. Blacks gave the example that you don't have to assimilate. You could do your own thing, get into your own background, your own history, your own tradition and your own culture." This insistence on the right of a people to articulate their own aesthetic vision had, as Reed notes, far-reaching effects.

Nevertheless, as a black woman married to a white man and the parent of a biracial daughter, Walker was considered suspect by this group, which was closely allied with the Black Nationalist movement. Her willingness to represent the failings of blacks as well as their good qualities did not endear her to the movement, either, and her respect in the white critical community was considered suspect by other writers, some of whom may have resented that respect.

Walker came to maturity as a writer during a fertile and exciting time in American literature, particularly for black women writers. When *The Color Purple* was published in 1982, it was part of a massive wave of work by black women writers that fundamentally changed the face of American literature by insisting on the literary worth not just of the black experience generally, but of the black woman's experience particularly. Walker and her colleagues challenged the literary dominance of the "everyman"—white and male—with their courageous and spirited heroines.

anties you got on." Just as quick as that, Miss Shug turne
se, let 'em drop to the ground, and with her foot flippe
nties over to Ma-Ma, who put them in her pocket. My gran
 looked over and said, "Ooh, give me them pretty pin
s you got on." Just as quick as that, Miss Shug turned '
let 'em drop to the ground, and with her foot flipped tl
s over to Ma-Ma, who put them in her pocket. My gran
 looked over and said, "Ooh, give me them pretty pin
s you got on." Just as quick as that, Miss Shug turned '
let 'em drop to the ground, and with her foot flipped tl
s over to Ma-Ma, who put them in her pocket. My gran
 looked over and said, "Ooh, give me them pretty pin
s you got on." Just as quick as that, Miss Shug turned '
let 'em drop to the ground, and with her foot flipped tl
s over to Ma-Ma, who put them in her pocket. My gran
 looked over and said, "Ooh, give me them pretty pin
s you got on." Just as quick as that, Miss Shug turned '
let 'em drop to the ground, and with her foot flipped tl
s over to Ma-Ma, who put them in her pocket. My gran
 looked over and said, "Ooh, give me them pretty pin
s you got on." Just as quick as that, Miss Shug turned '
let 'em drop to the ground, and with her foot flipped tl
s over to Ma-Ma, who put them in her pocket. My gran
 looked over and said, "Ooh, give me them pretty pin
s you got on." Just as quick as that, Miss Shug turned '
let 'em drop to the ground, and with her foot flipped tl
s over to Ma-Ma, who put them in her pocket. My gran
 looked over and said, "Ooh, give me them pretty pin
s you got on." Just as quick as that, Miss Shug turned '
let 'em drop to the ground, and with her foot flipped tl
s over to Ma-Ma, who put them in her pocket. My gran
 looked over and said, "Ooh, give me them pretty pin
s you got on." Just as quick as that, Miss Shug turned '
let 'em drop to the ground, and with her foot flipped tl
s over to Ma-Ma, who put them in her pocket. My gran
 looked over and said, "Ooh, give me them. pretty pin
s you got on." Just as quick as that, Miss Shug turned '
let 'em drop to the ground, and with her foot flipped tl
s over to Ma-Ma, who put them in her pocket. My gran
 looked over and said, "Ooh, give me them pretty pin
s you got on." Just as quick as that, Miss Shug turned
let 'em drop to the ground, and with her foot flipped tl

Part II:
Walker's Work

THIS POSTER FOR THE MOVIE VERSION OF *THE COLOR PURPLE* BECAME ONE OF THE MOST RECOGNIZABLE IMAGES OF THE 1980s AND BEYOND.

Chapter 1

The Color Purple

WALKER IS BEST KNOWN FOR HER 1982 NOVEL *The Color Purple*. In it she focuses on Celie, a young black woman in the Jim Crow South. Celie is poor and uneducated. She is unattractive and is sexually molested at a young age by a man she believes to be her father. She bears him two children who are taken from her, and then she is barren. She is trapped in a loveless marriage and a life of unending, brutally hard work. She is cruelly separated from her only living relation, her beloved sister Nettie, first by her marriage and then by her husband's amorous intentions toward her sister, and his cruel method of continuing to punish Celie for her sister's unwillingness to be his mistress.

Nevertheless Celie manages to create both meaning and community in her own small way. She surrounds herself with a variety of figures who teach her what it means to be strong: her husband's mistress, the beautiful blues singer Shug Avery; Sofia, the all-but-indomitable wife of her stepson Harpo; and eventually even long-lost Nettie, whose experiences as a missionary in Africa indicate both the promise of and limitations of Western religion and civilization.

Through Celie, Walker articulates a view of an ideal society in which men respect women, women respect themselves, and justice must inexorably assert itself. One might argue that this vision of community is idealistic, but Walker never suggests that such changes can happen without great trauma and effort.

Indeed the narrative of *The Color Purple*, an epistolary novel that spreads over a lifetime, tells of Celie's struggle to give up the fixed ideas that limit her horizons. She must learn that she has the right to her own property, her own sexuality, her own family, and her own identity. She must give herself permission to be angry at those who have wronged her, and to take the steps necessary to make herself happy. She moves from being a compliant slave to a strong business owner, breaking down barriers of gender with her unisex company Folkspants. And eventually, she even learns to forgive and talk to the man who took so much from her: her husband, Mr. _____.

At every step, Celie's greatest obstacles are her own ideas about what she "should" do, and unlearning damaging ideas handed down over generations about women's correct roles in society. Ultimately the book argues that men are as damaged and constrained by these roles as women are, and what must happen is not merely a destruction of patriarchal values, but a complete reorganization of roles based on personality and skill rather than gender. It is a bold project, and Walker's Celie, in many ways the most unlikely hero imaginable, makes it happen.

Background of the Writing

The Color Purple started as a rumination on Walker's family history.

Walker's grandfather, Henry Clay Walker, was in many ways the model for Mr. _____, as Celie refers to her brutal and uncaring husband, fearing even to call him by name. Like Mr. _____, Henry Walker had a lifetime passion for a singer named Shug, though his beloved singer was Shug Perry. Like Mr. _____, he was bullied by his father into dropping her in favor of a more respectable wife, but he continued to be unfaithful with Shug. As in the novel, the scorned wife took on a lover who objected when she tried to break off their affair. And like

Mr. _____, he then married a young, disempowered woman to care for his house and children. The young woman (Rachel) initially resented Shug, but then came to like her.

When the old man died in the 1970s, Walker returned home to pay her respects. Her sister Ruth told her a story: Miss Shug Perry used to visit the Walkers frequently, and one Sunday, walking home from church with her lover's wife Rachel and Rachel's granddaughter Ruth, they stopped at an outhouse, where Rachel noticed Shug's pink underpants.

> My grandmother looked over and said, "Ooh, give me them pretty pink panties you got on." Just as quick as that, Miss Shug turned 'em loose, let 'em drop to the ground, and with her foot flipped the panties over to Ma-Ma, who put them in her pocket. (White, 335)

Feeling sorry for Rachel, whose husband never gave her anything pretty, Shug Perry attempted to make up in some small way for the ongoing affair. This image, two women showing kindness to each other even though one is having an affair with the other's husband, seemed to Walker to be an affirmation of sisterhood. Walker had already addressed the agonies of the lover's triangle in her 1976 novel *Meridian*, but she noted a very different dynamic at play here: "I carried my sister's comment delicately balanced in the center of the novel's construction," she said (White, 336).

For this moment in her family history, Walker created a frame and peopled it with a collection of lively and interesting characters who first conform to the gender roles of the early twentieth century, then challenge them, articulating new roles and spaces for women and men and new relationships among them.

THE ROLE OF CELIE WAS PLAYED BY WHOOPI GOLDBERG IN THE 1985 MOVIE.

Principal Characters
Celie
Celie is the central character, and the author of most of—not all—the letters that make up the book. Celie is about thirteen when the novel begins, and it follows her through her adult life, ending when she is about sixty. Celie bears two children to her stepfather, and spends her life married to Mr. ____, raising his children, including Harpo. She has a brief lesbian affair with singer Shug Avery, but for most of the novel she is essentially asexual, at the center of a web of friends and family. She learns late in life that she is the owner of considerable property, and founds her own company, making unisex pants for men and women.

Nettie
Nettie is Celie's younger sister. She too suffers harassment at the hands of her stepfather, after which she moves in with Celie and Mr. _____. Mr. _____ has always been attracted to Nettie, however, and soon she must escape Celie's house as well. She moves in with the family of a black minister and his wife, who have adopted Celie's two children. She travels with the family to Africa, where she spends most of the novel, narrating the story of the colonization of the Olinka, an isolated tribe. Nettie returns only at the end of the novel with the widowed minister, now her husband, and Celie's adult children.

Mr. _____
A widower with four children, Mr. _____ is cruel to Celie because she fails on two counts: She is not Shug Avery, the true love whom Mr. _____'s domineering father would not allow him to wed, and she is not her sister Nettie, to whom he was also attracted. His first wife, Annie Julia, responded to his infidelity by having an affair of her own. When she attempted to break off that relationship, her lover shot her, and she died in her son's arms. Mr. _____

sees Celie primarily as a domestic slave: As the novel develops, he stops working his farm, leaving it to Harpo and Celie. Celie leaves him when she discovers that he has withheld from her many years' worth of letters from her sister. Later his son Harpo intervenes to restore his father to health and dignity, and he and Celie become companionable friends in their old age.

HERE, DANNY GLOVER AS ALBERT (MR. ____ IN THE NOVEL) SHAKES CELIE, TO WHOM HE IS NEEDLESSLY CRUEL.

Shug Avery

Shug Avery is a blues singer and model of strong black female sexuality. Before the time frame of the novel, she bore Mr. _____ two children. She fascinates Celie long before they meet, when Celie knows her only as her husband's mistress. When they meet, she is ill and cruel to Celie, who nevertheless takes good care of her and restores her to health. Shug and Celie become lovers, and Shug gives Celie different ways of understanding herself, her sexuality, her spirituality, and the world around her. Also, Mr. _____'s treatment of Celie causes Shug to lose interest in him as a partner. Celie never stops loving Shug, but their actual affair is fairly short. A singing job at Harpo's "juke joint" (a type of bar or nightclub) reestablishes her career and she becomes quite famous. She later marries Grady, then separates from him and takes up with Germaine, a much, much younger man.

Harpo

Harpo is the son of Mr. _____ and his first wife, Annie Julia. We first meet him just after Celie's wedding to Mr. _____, when he punishes Celie for not being his mother by throwing a stone at her head, which wounds her slightly. We also learn that his mother died in his arms, shot by her lover. He later marries Sofia, whose strength he both loves and resents. When Harpo asks Celie how to "make her mind," Celie replies, "Beat her." Harpo does, leading eventually to the disintegration of his marriage. He then opens a juke joint in his old house and has a relationship with a biracial woman named Squeak. After Celie leaves, Harpo develops a closer relationship with his father and is reunited with Sofia.

Sofia

Sofia is an enormous, and enormously strong, woman. She dates Harpo, but her father objects to him because of his mother's shameful death. She gets pregnant and they wed anyway, living in a small house on Mr. _____'s property and having several children. Harpo's attempts to control Sofia through violence cause her to beat him right back, and eventually she leaves, taking up with a boxer named Buster Broadnax. A condescending and insulting comment by the mayor's wife leads Sofia to strike the mayor, a crime for which she is imprisoned for many years, an experience she survives, she tells Celie, by "pretending I was you." Eventually, she is released to be a servant to the mayor and his family, and treated as a parent by the mayor's daughter, a role she resents. Toward the end of the novel, she is reunited with Harpo.

Squeak

Mary Agnes, known as Squeak by Harpo and his family, is a mixed-race young woman who lives with Harpo. We first meet her in the juke joint when she challenges Sofia, who knocks out two of her teeth. When Sofia is in prison, she helps raise Harpo's and Sofia's children. For Harpo's sake, she has sex with the prison warden to secure Sofia's release. At Shug's insistence, she becomes a singer as well, leaving Harpo to make a career. Eventually she enters into a relationship with Shug's husband Grady, based primarily around marijuana. They move to Central America to farm it, but then Squeak returns to the States and her career.

Grady

Grady is an auto mechanic who marries Shug Avery. He introduces Celie to "reefer," another word for marijuana. When Shug takes Celie away to Memphis, Grady and Squeak accompany them, eventually moving to Panama to farm marijuana. As Shug notes, "when you finish talking bout women and reefer, you finish Grady" (249).

Plot

The novel is told in a series of ninety letters, from the poor, ignorant Celie to God, from her sister Nettie back to Celie, and from Celie to Nettie. Celie takes literally her stepfather's injunction, "You better never tell nobody but God," a clear attempt to conceal his sexual abuse of Celie.

As the novel opens, Celie is questioning her own status as a moral person. "I am I have always been a good girl"(1). This strikethrough reveals that Celie has accepted that she is no longer good; she feels responsible for the wrongs done to her. She is pregnant, and she eventually has two children with Alphonso, whom she believes to be her father but is really her stepfather. Both of the children disappear, and she presumes they are dead. One day a local widower with four children comes to ask for the hand of Nettie, Celie's younger sister. Alphonso refuses to let Nettie go, but offers the widower Celie instead. The widower, Mr. _____, accepts the offer out of desperation. Mr. _____'s children are angry at their father for remarrying, and Harpo, the eldest son, attacks Celie immediately. To get through Mr. _____'s sexual advances, Celie concentrates on protecting Nettie.

One day in town, she sees a woman, the wife of a minister, with a young girl about the right age to be her daughter. She asks her the baby's name, and the woman tells her that the baby is called Pauline, but she calls her Olivia, the name Celie had embroidered on the baby's diapers before the child was taken away.

Celie's life at Mr. _____'s is drudgery, but she has no choice except to serve him. Nettie runs away from home to escape the attentions of Alphonso. She stays with Celie until Mr. _____ starts trying to seduce her, eventually trying to rape her. Celie sends her to the minister and his wife, "the only woman I ever seen with money"(18). Nettie goes to her, promising to write, but Celie does not hear from her again for nearly thirty years.

Shug Avery comes to town. Mr. _____ has been in love with Shug his whole life, but his father would not allow him to marry her. Instead he married Annie Julia, the mother of his four children, and continued his affair with Shug. Annie Julia also had an affair, but when she tried to break it off, feeling guilty, her lover shot her in front of her son, Harpo. She died in his arms.

Uninterested in Mr. _____ as a sexual partner, Celie finds herself drawn to Shug, whom she knows only from pictures. "Lord, I wants to go so bad. Not to dance. Not to drink. Not to play card. Not even to hear Shug Avery sing. I just be thankful to lay eyes on her."

Meanwhile Harpo has fallen in love with a strong-willed young woman named Sofia. Her father forbids their marriage, citing the death of Harpo's mother as evidence that the family is not worthy. Harpo intentionally impregnates her so that her father cannot object to their marriage. His father, on the other hand, dislikes Sofia, but she does not care. She tells Harpo that she will live with her sister and her husband until Harpo decides to be with them. Harpo fixes up a shed on his father's property and marries Sofia. She does not behave, however, like a traditional wife. When Harpo asks his father how to make her obey him, his father says to hit her. And when he asks Celie the same question, she answers, "Beat her." Sofia, however, fights back, and Harpo starts appearing with bruises and scratches.

Celie starts to regret her advice to Harpo, and when Sofia finds out that Celie was the one who told him to beat her, she confronts her. Celie tells Sofia that she envies her the ability to fight:

> She say, All my life I had to fight. I had to fight my daddy. I had to fight my brothers. I had to fight my cousins and my uncles. A girl child ain't safe in a family of men. But I never thought I'd have to

fight in my own house. She let out her breath. I loves Harpo, she say. God knows I do. But I'll kill him dead before I let him beat me. (40)

Celie, ashamed, apologizes to Sofia, who admits that she feels sorry for her, and encourages her to fight back against Mr. _____.

Shug Avery, ill, comes to stay at Mr. _____'s house. Celie nurses her back to health despite Shug's nasty comments. "She weak as a kitten. But her mouth just pack with claws" (49). Nevertheless, Celie feels drawn to Shug physically. As she gets healthier, she and Celie start to become friends.

Celie and Sofia start on a quilt called Sister's Choice. Celie works in pieces of a dress that Shug has donated. While they quilt, Sofia tells Celie that Harpo has started eating enormous amounts of food in an attempt to get to be as big as she is, so that his attempts to control her will have some effect. Sofia leaves him, going to live with her sister, a choice that causes Celie a pang of regret for her own lost sister.

When Sofia leaves, Harpo transforms their house into a juke joint, a small music club. It is not very successful until Shug starts to sing there. She writes a song for Celie, and then they become intimate when she discovers that Celie is essentially sexually innocent, making her look at herself naked. But Shug is planning on leaving soon, and spends every night with Mr. _____.

Sofia comes to the juke joint with her new boyfriend. Harpo's new girlfriend, a mixed-race woman called "Squeak," is angered when Harpo asks Sofia to dance; Squeak intervenes and they fight.

Soon after, Sofia is imprisoned for attacking the mayor. His wife, admiring her children, asks Sofia if she would be her maid. Sofia refuses, saying "Hell, no," so the mayor slaps her, and she hits him back. Celie and the others go to see Sofia in prison, where she has been badly beaten. She explains how she conforms to the prison routine: "Every time they ast me to do something, Miss Celie, I act like I'm you. I jump right up and do just what they say" (88). Squeak and Harpo take the children, but Sofia is clearly going insane in jail. They decide something must be done, so Squeak, the warden's niece, goes to intervene, allowing herself to be raped in exchange for Sofia's parole. But Sofia is not actually freed: She is sent to work at the mayor's house, the very fate she went to jail to avoid.

Meanwhile Squeak, who now insists that people use her given name of Mary Agnes, begins to sing in Shug's absence, first Shug's songs, and then her own.

Shug returns over the holidays with a new husband, Grady. He and Mr. _____ spend most of the time drinking together, leaving Shug and Celie alone. Celie confesses to Shug about her rape, and about Nettie. Shug tells Celie that she has seen Mr. _____ hiding letters, and they find them and read them.

Nettie did run to the minister, Samuel, and his wife. They educated her and took her with them to New York City and then to London, preparing to go to Africa as missionaries. The tribe with which they work, the Olinka, initially has had little contact with Americans, and none at all with people with black skin.

Although the Olinka have had some contact with Westerners, they have not been colonized. They worship their god, the roofleaf, upon which they depend for shelter and safety. When the missionaries arrive, they are presented with their own roof. They start a school, but only male students and Olivia attend. Olivia befriends an Olinka girl, Tashi. Her family does not approve of the friendship, but the girls endure. Nettie notes that Olinka men talk to women like the men at home do, as though they're invisible.

A road comes through the Olinka village, destroying the church, the school, and many dwellings and fields.

Soon, the entire village is transformed into a rubber plantation, and the Olinka become employees and tenants in their ancestral homeland.

Meanwhile, Corrine, Samuel's wife, is growing increasingly suspicious of Nettie, whom she believes to be Olivia and Adam's mother, because of the strong resemblance between them. It is through Corrine's suspicions that Nettie learns the truth: Alphonso is not her and Celie's father. Their real father was lynched because he was a successful black businessman, and their mother went mad. But Samuel, who as a young man had been a friend to Alphonso, took Celie's children and raised them as his own. When Nettie confesses her identity and connection to the children, Corrine is still bitter and angry, and her health fails. She finally relents and admits to meet Celie in town, but dies soon after.

Celie's anger at Mr. ____ for concealing the letters first makes her want to murder him, then leaves her feeling numb. Knowing that Nettie is alive, she now writes to her rather than God. Shug asks why, and Celie says that the God who lives in church—tall, white, white-haired—has never listened to her. Shug offers a different perspective, of a God who is inside people and nature, present in all things. She says all God wants is appreciation: "I think it pisses God off if you walk by the color purple in a field somewhere and don't notice it" (196). Celie hears her, but cannot believe. Shug decides that she must get Celie out of Georgia, and Celie curses Mr. ____ as she leaves. He responds: "You black, you pore, you ugly you a woman. Goddamn, he say, you nothing at all" (206). Celie replies, "I'm here" (207).

In Memphis, Celie lives in Shug's house and keeps her company. She also begins to make pants for people. She makes pants for Shug, for Squeak, and for Sofia's brother-in-law Jack. Soon everyone wants her pants, and she founds a company called Folkspants.

Celie returns to Georgia for Sofia's mother's funeral. There she sees Mr. ____, much improved, hard-working and clean. He had fallen into squalor after Celie left, but Harpo nursed him back to health. More important, he made Mr. ____ give up the rest of Nettie's letters to Celie.

When Nettie's letters continue, they tell of her marriage to the now-widowed Samuel, and of the destruction of the Olinka village and way of life. The family heads to England to try and raise relief money for the Olinka, but they fail. Samuel confesses to Nettie that he fears they have done nothing in Africa, that this is the fact that killed Corrine. Nettie points out that no one in Africa asked them to come; is it any surprise they are unwelcome? Samuel replies with tears in his eyes, "We love them. We try every way we can to show that love. But they reject us. They never even listen to how we've suffered. And if they listen they say stupid things. Why don't you speak our language? they ask. Why can't you remember the old ways? Why aren't you happy in America if everyone there drives motorcars?" (237). When they return to Africa, empty-handed, they discover that Tashi has undergone traditional Olinka facial scarification, in which the skin is sliced and objects such as sand are inserted underneath to form decorative textured ridges, and is hiding, because she is in love with Adam and doesn't want him to see her. She finally emerges, but soon she and her mother Catherine disappear, joining the Olinka who have run from the rubber plantation. Adam goes after her, and after nearly three months, returns with her. He has also scarred his face. Samuel marries them.

Back in America, Alphonso has died. The house he built with Celie's parents' money is hers (as was the money), and his young new wife has no interest in keeping it. Shug and Celie light incense to clear the evil spirits from the house.

HERE, CELIE TAKES A LOOK AT ONE OF THE SERIES OF LETTERS THAT
TELL THE STORY OF HER LIFE AND THOSE OF THE OTHER CHARACTERS IN
THE NOVEL AND SUBSEQUENT FILM.

But Shug has fallen in love with a young man, breaking Celie's heart. Grady and Squeak, now openly a couple, move to Panama to raise marijuana. Most importantly, however, Celie and Mr. _____ become friends. They talk about their marriage, about their shared love for Shug. They sew together.

Shug sends her young lover to college and returns to a peaceful scene with Celie and Mr. _____. Squeak returns to America to focus on her singing career. Nettie, Samuel, Adam, Olivia, and Tashi arrive, completing the circle of family.

Major Themes
Gender

Throughout her career, Walker's main concern has been the representation of black women, seeking to give voice to the voiceless, to those who suffer the double oppression of race and gender. Celie is, in many ways, Walker's archetypal heroine: Her path from oppression to anger to acceptance and wholeness comprises the narrative of *The Color Purple*.

Walker has long been criticized for what many consider to be her unfair portrayal of black men. There is some truth to this claim: In *The Color Purple* nearly every major male character—particularly Alphonso, Mr. _____, and Harpo—has significant problems relating to women as anything other than their personal possessions, to be used as they see fit. Alphonso marries an insane woman and proceeds to father two children on her daughter. Then, after her death, he marries a series of much younger women. Mr. _____, thwarted in his early love for Shug Avery, proceeds to punish first Annie Julia and then Celie for the crime of not being Shug. Harpo sacrifices a genuine passion for Sofia on the altar of gender hierarchy: It becomes more important to him to assert his manhood by controlling her rather than loving her. But Mr._____ and

Harpo gradually learn that their behavior alienates the women they love, and both reform, in their own ways.

Celie is far more comfortable with women than with men. "I don't even look at mens. I look at women, tho, cause I'm not scared of them" (5). Nevertheless, she is brutally raped by her stepfather and bears him two children, the latter of whom leaves her unable to bear children. She is also married off to a man she does not know or love. Late in the book, when Mr. _____ asks if Celie hates him because he is male, she says, "Take off they pants, I say, and men look like frogs to me. No matter how you kiss 'em, as far as I'm concern, frogs is what they stay" (254). And yet, their status as "frogs" would not prevent her liking them well enough, were they kind to her.

Instead the men of *The Color Purple* seem determined to make the women under them pay for the wrongs of society by enforcing strict gender divisions, often through violence. Their sexual appetites are voracious and often aimed inappropriately. And they seem unable to grant the women in their lives any right to make decisions for and about themselves. Notable exceptions to this rule are Samuel, who is kind and loving to his wife, his adopted children, and Nettie (though, when it counts, he declines to intervene to protect Celie); Sofia's boyfriend Buster Broadnax, who says "my job to love her and take her where she want to go" (82); and Jack, the husband of Sofia's sister Odessa, who is a model for stability and fatherly love. When Celie makes a pair of pants for Jack, she thinks that they must be strong and soft, with big pockets for toys, snug enough that he can run to rescue a child from danger, but also "something he can lay back in when he hold Odessa in front of the fire" (213). But these are all comparatively minor characters: The dominant male characters do not allow themselves these moments of tenderness.

NETTIE AND THE YOUNG CELIE PLAY IN A FIELD OF FLOWERS
BEFORE NETTIE MUST LEAVE FOR AFRICA.

Sexual intercourse in the novel tends to be presented as rape or abuse: Celie tells Shug that Mr. _____ just "do his business, get off, go to sleep," to which Shug replies, "Why Miss Celie! You make it sound like he going to the toilet on you." Celie answers "That what it feel like" (77). Similarly, when Harpo is most determined to exercise his power over Sofia, his attitude affects their sex life. "Once he git on top of me I think bout how that's where he always want to be" (65). Clearly the lack of equity in these relationships affects how the couples interact.

Instead, Walker seems to suggest, what women need is knowledge of their own bodies, someone to treat them gently and teach them about more than having babies. What Shug offers Celie, more than anything else, is knowledge of herself. And Shug's gentleness, her assurance to Celie that sexuality is beautiful and blessed, helps restore Celie to wholeness. Walker has been criticized for suggesting that lesbianism is an answer to the problems between men and women; this criticism is, at least in Celie's case, unfounded.

Instead, Walker offers another model for male-female relations. With the exception of the unrepentant Alphonso, the major male characters eventually learn to give up their desires to control the women in their lives and accept their strength and equality. Once Celie gathers the courage to walk out on Mr.____, he first falls into squalor and madness, but is then rescued by his son Harpo.

Harpo, having lost Sofia and then Squeak, wins back his wife by refusing to conform to traditional male roles and nursing his father back to health. Sofia tells Celie, "Well, one night I walked up to tell Harpo something— and the two of them was just laying there on the bed fast asleep. Harpo holding his daddy in his arms. After that, I start to feel again for Harpo." When Celie asks how Mr. ____ was restored to sanity, Sofia replies "Harpo made him send you the rest of your sister's letters. Right after that, he start to improve. You know how meanness kill, she say" (223–224). Thus it is only when Mr. ____ stops punishing Celie that he can be restored to himself.

The most improbable and hopeful friendship in the novel, the one that offers the greatest hope for social cohesion, develops at last between Celie and Mr. ____. He confesses to her that:

> You used to remind me of a bird. Way back when you first come and live with me. You was so skinny, Lord, he say. And the least little thing happen, you looked about to fly away.
> You saw that, I say.
> I saw it, he said, just too big a fool to let myself care. (253)

Celie recognizes the change in Mr. _____, and rewards him with her friendship:

> After all the evil he done, I know you wonder why I don't hate him. I don't hate him for two reasons. One, he love Shug. And two, Shug use to love him. Plus, look like he trying to make something out himself. I don't mean just that he work and he clean up after himself and he appreciate some of the things God was playful enough to make. I mean when you talk to him now he really listen, and one time, out of nowhere in the conversation us was having, he said Celie, I'm satisfied this is the first time I ever lived on earth as a natural man. It feel like a new experience. (260)

This often-overlooked section elevates Mr. _____'s character. He is no longer the one-dimensional perpetrator punishing the sympathetic victim—he is revealed as complex and sensitive in his own right. When Celie stops being a victim, he loses himself, but then finds himself again as a "natural man," treating himself and the world with love and respect. When that relationship is established, Walker strongly suggests, equity and harmony between the genders will follow.

Religion

One of Walker's major concerns in *The Color Purple* is the representation of religion. God is an important character in the book: The vast majority of the letters included are addressed to him. But Celie loses her faith altogether when Mr. _____'s betrayal with Nettie's letters is revealed, inspiring one of Walker's most direct refashionings of the traditional idea of religion.

Celie believes that God is a white man: "He big and old and tall and graybearded and white. He wear white robes and go barefooted." Shug agrees: "Ain't no way to read the bible and not think God white. . . . When I find out I thought God was white, and a man, I lost interest. You mad cause he don't seem to listen to your prayers. Humph! Do the mayor listen to anything colored say?" (194 –195).

Instead Shug proposes an ideal of religion based on the idea that God exists through and inside of people and things, rather than as an abstract, judgmental creator: "I believe God is everything, say Shug" (195).

> She say, My first step from the old white man was trees. Then air. Then birds. Then other people. But one day when I was sitting quiet and feeling like a motherless child, which I was, it come to me: that feeling of being a part of everything, not separate at all. I knew that if I cut a tree, my arm would bleed. And I laughed and I cried and I run all around the house. I knew just what it was. In fact, when it happen, you can't miss it. It sort of like you know what, she say, grinning and rubbing high up on my thigh.
> Shug! I say
> Oh, she say. God love all them feelings That's some of the best stuff God did. And when you know God loves 'em, you enjoys 'em a lot more. You can just relax, go with everything that's going, and praise God by doing what you like. (196)

After connecting God explicitly to sexuality, Shug notes, "I think it pisses God off when you walk by the color purple in a field somewhere and don't notice it" (196), indicating the centrality of this important theme in the novel.

Race

Explicit discussions of race play a small part in *The Color Purple*. It's not that race is irrelevant; it's just that there are few significant white characters, so the encounters between white and black culture are limited. Black culture is presented largely as a closed system, only touching on white culture when absolutely necessary, usually as an unreasonable and unreasoning source of violent authority.

The events surrounding Sofia's imprisonment offer the clearest illustration of encounters with white society. In this altercation, the mayor's wife makes a condescending compliment to Sofia, then asks if she would like to work as her maid. Clearly the woman believes her offer to be a tremendous compliment, and is shocked at Sofia's response: "Hell, no." The mayor gets involved and slaps Sofia for her presumption, so she strikes him in return.

> When I see Sofia, I don't know why she still alive. They crack her skull, they crack her ribs. They tear her nose loose on one side. They blind her in one eye. She swole from head to foot. Her tongue the size of my arm, it stick out tween her teef like a piece of rubber. She can't talk. And she just about the color of a eggplant. (86–87)

Obviously these injuries were not bestowed by the mayor, but by law enforcement. Once Sofia is in the hands of white society, violence is expected. (It's worth noting that Celie, at least, blames Sofia's arrest on Harpo: "If you hadn't tried to rule over Sofia, the white folks never would have caught her" (200).)

Even the whites who claim the greatest affection for blacks seem unable to comprehend the very simple fact that blacks are human beings. Miss Millie, the mayor's wife, for example, tells Sofia that she can have Christmas with her family, but because of her poor driving skills and racism against black men (she refuses to allow Jack, Odessa's husband, to drive her home when her car gets stuck), Sofia's "treat" consists of driving Miss Millie around and spending a few minutes with her children.

Similarly Miss Millie's daughter Eleanor Jane claims the greatest affection for Sofia, but her concerns seem generally to be with forcing Sofia to admire her husband and then her baby. Sofia must put her down sharply for her to realize that Sofia's concerns are not her concerns, and that their relationship was always one of compulsion rather than affection. Eleanor Jane, however, reforms somewhat, and goes to great lengths to help Henrietta, Harpo, and Sofia's youngest daughter, who has sickle-cell anemia.

As with divisions between the genders, divisions between races, Walker implies, can only be healed when both parties can consider each other as equals.

Significant Elements
The Form of the Novel
An *epistolary* novel is one in which the text is organized not (or not only) through a standard arrangement of chapters, but rather through a series of letters. The form has a long tradition in English-language literature, most famously Bram Stoker's *Dracula*.

Many of the earliest novels in English were written in the epistolary form, but the style largely fell out of favor by the mid-nineteenth century. The epistolary form offers the authenticity of a first-person narrative voice, with the reader looking in upon a private correspondence.

The Color Purple is an unusual epistolary novel in many ways. For example, epistolary novels often involve an exchange between two or more people. In *The Color Purple*, the intended recipients are either supernatural—and so will not answer the letters written to them—or presumed by the writer not to receive the letters sent. As Nettie notes:

> I remember one time you said your life made you feel so ashamed you couldn't even talk about it to God, you had to write it, bad as you thought your writing was. Well, now I know what you meant. And whether God will read letters or no, I know you will go on writing them; which is guidance enough for me. Anyway, when I don't write to you I feel as bad as when I don't pray, locked up in myself and choking on my own heart. I am so *lonely*, Celie. (130)

In this novel, then, the characters write because they have to make a connection with the outside world for themselves, not because they expect a response.

The letters in *The Color Purple* are generally organized by author and recipient: Celie to God, Nettie to Celie, Celie to Nettie. As such, they are first-person narratives told from particular characters' points of view, and thus limited first-person perspective. For example, Celie, who does not know until late in the novel that Alphonso is not her father, calls him Pa throughout, and believes Olivia and Adam to be her siblings as well as her children. She genuinely believes Nettie to be dead for much of the book. Although she owns property, she does not know it, and so she believes herself to be destitute and completely dependent upon Mr. _____. We only know what Celie knows, what Nettie knows.

Another important aspect of this epistolary novel in particular is the confused timeline created by the concealment of Nettie's letters, arguably the cruelest thing Mr. _____ does to Celie. Thus, though Nettie's trip to Africa occurs during the early days of Celie's marriage, Celie (and we) do not learn of it until many years later.

The reader must then create two timelines—one of Celie's experiences and one of Nettie's—and work them together. The most vivid example of this in the novel is when Nettie notes that she has seen a woman serving the mayor's wife who looks like she should not be serving anyone: That's Sofia, and the fact that Nettie sees her as a servant forces the reader to readjust perceptions of the relationship between events in the novel's timeline.

Dialect

The Color Purple is written primarily in dialect, which varies according to the educational level of the person writing. Since Celie's voice dominates the book, the story is told mostly in her rural Georgia dialect. But Nettie's educated, religious tones, the gritty language of the juke joint, Shug's transcendent and philosophical appreciation of nature, all have their own tone and form.

Critical Response

Almost immediately upon publication, *The Color Purple* was recognized as a masterwork of American literature. Its unusual form and language, as well as the risky nature of the narrative, struck a chord for many critics, who lauded its creativity and liveliness.

Mel Watkins, writing in the *New York Times*, called Walker "A lavishly gifted writer," and noted particularly the narrative style of the epistolary novel in folk dialect:

> What makes Miss Walker's exploration so indelibly affecting is the choice of a narrative style that, without the intrusion of the author, forces intimate identification with the heroine. Most of the letters that comprise this epistolary novel are written by Celie, although correspondence from Netti

[sic] is included in the latter part of the book. Initially, some readers may be put off by Celie's knothole view of the world, particularly since her letters are written in dialect and from the perspective of a naive, uneducated adolescent. . . . As the novel progresses, however, and as Celie grows in experience, her observations become sharper and more informed; the letters take on authority and the dialect, once accepted, assumes a lyrical cadence of its own. . . . The cumulative effect is a novel that is convincing because of the authenticity of its folk voice. And, refreshingly, it is not just the two narrator-correspondents who come vividly alive in this tale. A number of memorable female characters emerge. There is Shug Avery, whose pride, independence and appetite for living act as a catalyst for Celie and others, and Sofia, whose rebellious spirit leads her not only to desert her overbearing husband but also to challenge the social order of the racist community in which she lives.

Similarly effusive praise came from Peter Prescott, in *Newsweek*, who called the book a work of "permanent importance." He continues, "Her story begins at about the point that a respectable Greek tragedy reserves for its climax . . . then works its way toward acceptance, serenity, and joy."

Novelist Rita Mae Brown found the book more personal than that: "When you close the book, you will be left with your own heartbeat. . . . It is a work to stand beside literature from any time and place. It needs no category other than the fact that it is superb."

Millions of readers around the world have confirmed what these critics saw in the text: Celie's story remains as popular and vibrant today as it was over twenty years ago. The novel's readers share in Celie's trauma, but also in her triumph, and the world she inhabits strikes true. Few books can claim both critical and popular appeal, but *The Color Purple* does so.

The Color Purple on Film

Some novels take many years before their artistry and message become generally accepted. Not *The Color Purple*, which had an immediate impact, winning the National Book Award and Pulitzer Prize almost immediately. Similarly, the process of adapting the novel for the screen began shortly after its publication, and the book has since been readapted as a Broadway musical (which will also be made into a film, currently in preproduction).

The Color Purple Movie (1985)

One of the difficulties of translating modern literary works for the screen is that such narratives tend to focus on the protagonist's perspective as a literary device. Filming such narratives presents an obvious difficulty. We experience the novel through Celie's eyes, with her information and interpretations, but short of having the camera act as an eye with a voice-over, there's no way to translate such a perspective-based story effectively on film. When adapting such works for the screen, then, something is inevitably lost, and the focus shifts to the events of the plot.

The film version of *The Color Purple* owes its existence primarily to music producer Quincy Jones, who acted as intermediary between Walker and director Steven Spielberg. At the time, Spielberg was famous primarily for the mega-blockbuster *ET: The Extra Terrestrial* (1982). Walker had significant misgivings about Spielberg: She felt that a white, male director could not understand or translate her work effectively. But Spielberg was persistent and asked Walker to help adapt her own novel, assuaging many of her concerns. As she reportedly said to her daughter, "Maybe if he can do Martians, he can do us" (Dworkin). As one film critic argued, Spielberg may not have been a perfect director, but he alone may have been able to get the film made: As a prominent (and commercially successful) director, he had clout, and he used it for *The Color Purple* (Canby).

The production was hampered by controversy, generally focusing on two issues: the representation of black men in the film and the role of lesbianism as part of Celie's broader awakening of consciousness and self-confidence.

The first of these issues had long been a debate within black women's writing. I note elsewhere in this volume the case of Ntozake Shange, whose play *For Colored Girls Who Have Considered Suicide When the Rainbow Is Enuf* (1975) had been attacked on similar grounds. Shange and Walker were friends, and Walker knew how brutal such criticism could be. In her own first novel, *The Third Life of Grange Copeland*, the character Brownfield was also an unrepentant figure of violence and anger. And certainly many of the major male characters in *The Color Purple* come off pretty badly, from the rape and injunction to silence of Celie's stepfather Alphonso with which the text begins, to the callous disregard and active cruelty of Mr. _____, to Harpo's desperate and ultimately destructive attempts to make his wife Sofia "mind." However, in the novel, many of these characters ultimately can be seen as trapped by a system that is as dangerous for them as for the women they oppress. Harpo allows himself to become nurturing, Mr. _____'s anger is revealed as a symptom of his love for Shug Avery, and he even learns to sew and becomes friends with Celie.

In the film, much of this character development is jettisoned in favor of a focus on Celie's progress. In isolation, that is not a problem—filmmakers often simplify narratives and reduce the importance of supporting characters—but in this case it leaves both Harpo and Mr._____ essentially unchanged. It is true that Harpo reunites with Sofia in the film, but only as part of a broader formation of community, and only after her will has been broken by imprisonment and service. And Mr._____ has a moment of peculiar generosity, in which he produces money to help Nettie and her family return to the United States, but he himself is never reintegrated into the family.

Many African-American critics pointed to these narrative shifts as telling moments of collusion between Walker and her white producer and director, with the supposed purpose of scapegoating black men for the problems of black women. Jacqueline Bobo concisely summed up the controversy: "Tony Brown, a syndicated columnist and the host of the television program *Tony Brown's Journal* has called the film *The Color Purple* 'the most racist depiction of Black men since *The Birth of a Nation* and the most anti-Black family film of the modern film era.' Ishmael Reed, a Black novelist, has labeled the film and the book 'a Nazi conspiracy.'" Such strong language indicates the depth of the responses the film engendered.

Others have defended the film, noting that Walker's book, and the film made from it, are works of art and not intended to be disinterested representations of the black experience in America. More important, black women have argued that the film represents an important step forward for them. Jacqueline Bobo cites author Donald Bogle, who notes the novelty of *The Color Purple* for many viewers, despite their recognition of the film's flaws. Bogle notes that some black viewers might have a "schizophrenic reaction" to the film, recognizing the stereotypes of black men, but respecting the representation of black women:

> You have never seen Black women like this put on the screen before. I'm not talking about what happens to them in the film, I'm talking about the visual statement itself. When you see Whoopi Goldberg in close-up, a loving close-up, you look at this woman, you know that in American films in the past, in the 1930s, 1940s, she would have played a maid. She would have been a comic maid. Suddenly, the camera is focusing on her and we say I've seen this woman some place, I know her.

From our contemporary perspective, it's hard to believe that when the film was released Whoopi Goldberg and Oprah Winfrey were young unknowns. Their portrayals (and that of Margaret Avery as Shug) redefined the way black women were presented on film. In that respect, the film is true to Walker's vision of creating a strong female-centered black community.

However, in another sense, the film belies the intensity of Walker's perspective, particularly in the almost complete excision of the lesbian content of the novel. The duration of Celie and Shug's actual sexual relationship in the novel is short, but its effects on Celie are permanent. Growing up to believe that sex was punishment, Celie desperately needs Shug to restore her respect for her own body as part of the natural world. And though some may be squeamish about the topic, Walker chose to accomplish this particular narrative task in the novel by means of awakening Celie's sexuality.

There are any number of reasons the sexual relationship between Celie and Shug might have been removed from the film. In our culture, female sexuality, if it's represented at all, tends to be seen through the eye of an imagined male viewer. But though Celie, who was raped, was a parent, and was married, she was never loved as a woman for herself. Shug's love is healing. When Celie describes Mr. _____'s sexual contact to Shug, the latter notes, "You make it sound like he going to the toilet on you" (77). Although the film has some sexual elements, they are far more muted, and a generalized female bonding replaces the erotic relationship, making Celie's love for Shug less profound and particular: Shug is just one of several women who affect Celie. As Walker noted in her book *The Same River Twice*, "In the movie almost all the women kiss each other, making the kiss between Celie and Shug less significant" (168). Thus the role of lesbian sexuality as being personally and politically transformative is largely absent from the film.

Even in its merely suggestive form, however, the lesbian content of the film caused a great deal of controversy. A group called the Coalition Against Black Exploitation was particularly virulent, concerned that "homosexuality is not projected to the masses as a solution to the problems that Black men and women face with each other." Such alarms had a clear effect on the final product; producer Quincy Jones assured the head of the Coalition, Earl Walter Jr., that the love scenes would be "tasteful," and in fact, the contact consisted solely of a single kiss.

Other issues critics had with the film included what many perceived to be an unnecessary softening of the grittiness of Walker's narrative: No one is really poor in the film, and violence is suggested rather than shown. Visually, the film is lush, and beautiful. Although certainly there are moments in the text in which the beauty of nature presents itself as an important element (particularly in Shug and Celie's conversation about the nature of God and the color purple), in the film, pastoral imagery dominates, concealing or at least overwhelming the often grim nature of the narrative.

A further point of contention is the representation of Sofia, whose presence in the text continually challenges Celie's trauma-survivor ideas about how men and women should behave toward one another. Sofia is in many ways the most tragic character in the novel: Wrongfully punished, she suffers from the attentions of the almost invisible white culture in a way no one else in the novel does. Her relationship with Harpo is fraught with the tension between love and self-respect. Yet in the film, a young Oprah Winfrey plays Sofia for laughs. She's heavy, but she's not powerful, just amusing. And Harpo fares even worse: "Barbara Christian found the most maligned figure in the film to be Harpo. She said that in the book he couldn't become the patriarch that society demanded that he become. Because the film cannot depict a man uncomfortable with the requirements of patriarchy, Harpo is made into a buffoon. Christian adds that 'the movie makes a negative statement about men who show some measure of sensitivity to women.'" Michele Wallace, who sees the Sofia/Harpo dynamic as a series of "white patriarchal interventions" went further:

In the book Sofia is the epitome of a woman with masculine powers, the martyr to sexual injustice who eventually triumphs through the realignment of the community. In the movie she is an occasion for humor. She and Harpo are the reincarnation of Amos and Sapphire; they alternately fight their way to a house full of pickaninnies. Harpo is always falling through the roof he's chronically unable to repair. Sofia is always shoving a baby into his arms, swinging her large hips, and talking a mile a minute. Harpo, who is dying to marry Sofia in the book, seems bamboozled into marriage in the film. Sofia's only masculine power is her contentiousness. Encircled by the mayor, his wife and an angry white mob, she is knocked down and her dress flies up providing us with a timely reminder that she is just a woman.

The changes in Sofia and Harpo, then, represent a weakening of their characters, making them parody rather than tragedy.

Despite its numerous flaws, however, the film was incredibly popular, particularly considering the subject matter. It was nominated for eleven Oscars; although it did not win any, it did win a number of other awards. And it remains an enjoyable film with excellent performances, particularly from the lead actors, many of whom have gone on to have decades of success in other roles.

The Color Purple (stage musical, 2005)

Music is an important part of *The Color Purple*, so in some ways, its adaptation as a stage musical seemed pre-ordained. When the show previewed in Atlanta in 2004, critic Jim Farmer noted a marked difference from the film: "The musical embraces the lesbian content of the book much more overtly than the film. Shug's duet with Celie, 'What About Love'—sung near the end of the first act after Celie has fallen for her—is a beautiful moment, the first time the show really feels alive." Once the play hit Broadway in 2005, reviews were mixed, most noting that it seemed rushed, as though events were overtaking characters before they had time to develop. Even more than film, stage drama requires a simple narrative, and *The Color Purple* is not simple.

The play owes its existence to actress and celebrity Oprah Winfrey, who put much of her clout behind it. The cast changed multiple times between 2004 and 2008, something not unusual on Broadway, but *The Color Purple* was notable partly because so many of its cast

MR. _____ HAS QUITE AN EFFECT ON THE LADIES. HERE, HE TAKES A BREAK FROM HIS DAY JOB.

members were famous from other venues, such as popular music (Michelle Williams) or shows such as *American Idol* (Fantasia Barrino).

One of the most marked shifts in the play is the role of the chorus, who act, as in Greek literature, partly as characters in the drama, and partly as commentators on the events. The Ladies of the Church and Mr._____'s Field Hands represent conventional wisdom about men and women, morality and immorality, and the right relationship between people. From the perspective of the play, they are often wrong, of course, but their opinions help contextualize Celie's crises and development.

The Color Purple's Broadway run closed in the spring of 2008, but the show continues to tour. It is expected to be made into a film, currently slated for release in 2010.

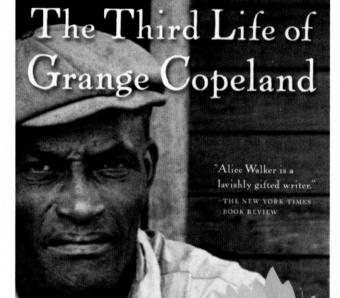

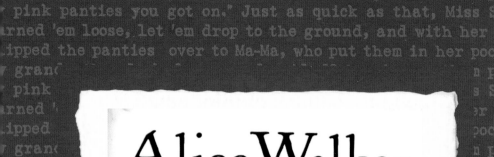

Alice Walker

Pulitzer Prize-winning author of THE COLOR PURPLE

The Third Life of Grange Copeland

"Alice Walker is a
lavishly gifted writer."

—THE NEW YORK TIMES
BOOK REVIEW

THE THIRD LIFE OF GRANGE COPELAND WAS WALKER'S FIRST NOVEL,
BUT ITS THEMES WERE TO RESONATE IN MUCH OF HER LATER WORK.

Chapter 2

Other Novels

ALTHOUGH *THE COLOR PURPLE* is by far Walker's best-known novel, the concerns raised in it are consistent with those of her other works, particularly her other novels.

The Third Life of Grange Copeland

Walker's first novel, *The Third Life of Grange Copeland* (1970), focuses on the history of a sharecropping family in the South in order to illuminate the causes of, responses to, and possible solutions to the problem of entrenched racial injustice.

In the novel, which follows the Copeland family through three generations, Walker tells the story of Grange, his son Brownfield, and Brownfield's daughter Ruth. Grange (the name clearly indicates the rural, agricultural history of much of the Southern black experience), transfers the abuse he receives at the hands of the white landowner Shipley to his wife and child. He first engages in public infidelity with a prostitute, and then escapes from his family to New York. His wife, Margaret, commits suicide.

Meanwhile, Brownfield (the name points to the barren nature of the life he leads) marries Mem (whose name is the French *la meme*, which means "the same," indicating the repetition of patterns of abuse), an educated schoolteacher he comes to resent and bully. She resists his control, even drawing a shotgun on him at one point to defend herself against a beating. But her self-defense is short-lived: An uncongenial husband, many children, and the crushing grind of poverty conspire to break her health and spirit. Even then, Brownfield is plagued by fears that Mem is unfaithful to him and that her degrading (given her education) position as a domestic servant, or maid, makes public his own inability to provide for his family, so he murders her.

In New York, Brownfield's father, encountering a terrified, pregnant white woman in Central Park, allows her to drown when she runs away because she is afraid of him as a black man. The anger springing from this event releases all his pent-up rage, and he attacks whites indiscriminately for a time. However, the violence he unleashes upon those who are, after all, not personally responsible for his suffering leads to a broader consideration of the issues of race and hatred. His conscience starts to bother him, and he decides that self-love and self-respect are the way forward, not hatred and violence.

Grange returns to the South, to his son and grandchildren. After a metaphorical death, he develops a close relationship with his granddaughter Ruth, and attempts to heal his son's broken soul. "The white folks hated me and I hated myself in return. Then I tried just loving me, and then you, and then ignoring them as much as I could," he says to her (196). It is this life, his third, that leaves open the possibility of redemption: Ruth approaches the world through love of self, not hatred of others, and as such represents the best hope for a way forward. Such a move, however, requires the destruction of the tyrannical Brownfield, indicating the cost of advancement.

The Third Life of Grange Copeland is a novel deeply concerned with the idea of self-determination, particularly as it relates to questions of blame and guilt. The two central characters, Grange and Brownfield Copeland, are both victims of racism. Both respond to the frustrations of their lives with violence. Walker outlines how the cycle of violence begins, with Grange and then Brownfield seeing in violence the only possible response to oppression.

But, Walker suggests, such a response to oppression is ultimately a dead-end. It continues a destructive cycle and does nothing to right the original wrong. The crucial thing is to be strong, to take responsibility for one's own actions, and to try to end injustice rather than perpetuate it. As Grange says to his son:

> I *know* the danger of putting all the blame on somebody else for the mess you make out of your life. I fell into the trap myself! And I'm bound to believe that that's the way the white folks can corrupt you even when you done held up before. 'Cause when they got you thinking that they're to blame for *every* thing they have you thinking they's some kid of gods! You can't do nothing wrong without them being behind it. . . . Nobody's as powerful as we make them out to be. We got our own *souls*, don't we? (207)

Grange takes responsibility for his own actions, for his mistreatment of his wife, and for his neglect of his son. But he believes that Brownfield should take responsibility for himself too: "But when he become a man himself, with his own opportunity to righten the wrong I done him by being good to his own children, he had the chance to become a real man. . . . But he messed up with his children, his wife and his home, and he never yet blamed hisself" (206). Grange then intercedes on behalf of his beloved granddaughter: "You can't just take this young girl here and make her wish she was dead just to git back at some white folks you don't even *know*" (209). The cycle of violence, Walker argues, must end.

In her afterword to the book, Walker made this plea explicit: "The white man's oppression of me will never excuse my oppression of you, whether you are a man, woman, child, animal, or tree. Because the self I prize refuses to be owned by him. Or by anyone." Nevertheless many critics misunderstood the book, preferring to focus on its violence rather than its ultimate message of peace through self-love. Such a misreading is probably not surprising: By 1970 the Black Nationalist movement was politically prominent, and groups such as the Black Panthers were perceived by some as menacing white America, much as the unreformed Grange had menaced New York City. Walker struck back harshly at one critic who misread the book in this way, noting particularly the critic's "declaration that my main character cures himself of self-hatred 'presumably' by beating up as many white people as he can. This insults my imagination, and it is ridiculous besides. . . . However, it simply happens that in this novel what motivates the old man to change is love of self (not love or hatred of white folks. . . .)" (cited in White, 190). She sent this letter to many of her friends and mentors, with a cover note that argued for the importance of responding to such readings: "It is imperative that black artists protest racist interpretations of their work, cavalier and insensitive handling of it, and white people's unfailing ability to be dishonest, when it comes to evaluating the work of black artists" (cited in White, 190).

The troubling narrative of *The Third Life of Grange Copeland* prefigured many of the important themes Walker would explore in her later work: the inheritance of violence and anger from generation to generation, the compounding of externally imposed suffering by internal acts, and the redemptive power of family and connection, particularly as it applies to women. When the Copeland family manages to stop destroying their women in the name of the suffering of their men, the way forward is clear.

Meridian

In *Meridian* (1976), Walker creates a character whose life path closely follows what her own might have been. Like Walker, Meridian Hill is a young black woman, educated at a traditional women's college, active in the civil rights

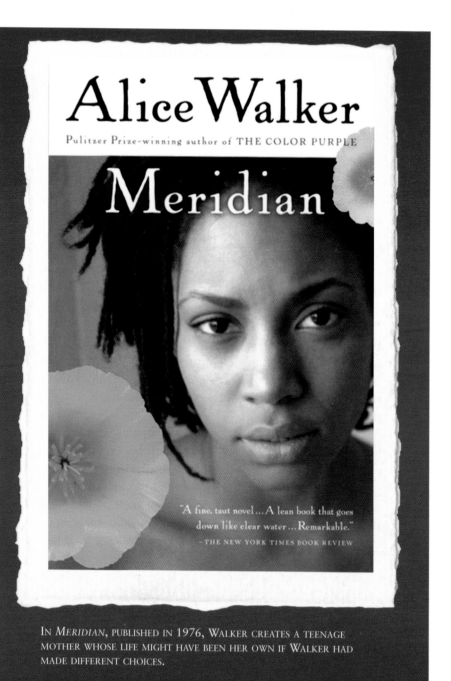

IN *MERIDIAN*, PUBLISHED IN 1976, WALKER CREATES A TEENAGE MOTHER WHOSE LIFE MIGHT HAVE BEEN HER OWN IF WALKER HAD MADE DIFFERENT CHOICES.

movement, who gets involved with one of her fellow activists. But Meridian is a teenage mother who leaves her child to the care of relatives in order to pursue her education. She is an agitator for justice at her college. She chooses to live among the poor and dispossessed, and her struggle for authenticity takes a brutal physical toll on her.

Meridian is a nonlinear narrative about the political and personal development of a young civil rights activist. It begins with Truman Held, a black civil rights activist, going to Chicokema, Georgia, to meet with his ex-lover, Meridian. She is intervening—literally facing down a tank—so that young black children can see a traveling mummy in a freak show. The effort of this intervention makes her pass out, a physical symptom that appears to be related to epilepsy and was shared by her father and great-grandmother. Truman takes her back to her dingy digs, and tells her he still thinks of her often. The novel then flashes back to a political meeting where Meridian refuses to commit murder in the name of revolution; to her estrangement from her mother because of her mother's stringent Christianity; to the events surrounding the death of the Wild Child, a homeless, pregnant teen living around Saxon College who Meridian tries to help, and when she can't, to bury respectfully. Other flashbacks include an encounter with a sublime, otherworldly presence at an ancient Cherokee burial mound called the Sacred Serpent Mound where she has her first fainting spells, Meridian's recollections of her untimely pregnancy and early marriage, and her experiences at Saxon College, a thinly veiled representation of Spelman.

The core of the book is a love triangle between Meridian, Truman Held, and Lynne Rabinowitz, a white Jewish woman from the North who comes to the South to assist with civil rights work such as voter registration and education. Meridian is an ambivalent revolutionary, Truman a committed (if self-centered) artist, and Lynne determined to undo three hundred years of racial injustice on her own. Truman first becomes Meridian's lover, then Lynne's. In the face of his indecision and her own goals, Meridian aborts a pregnancy and has a tubal ligation, so she cannot become pregnant again. Truman, married to Lynne and a father of a daughter, nevertheless continues to gravitate toward Meridian. As the political situation worsens for the civil rights workers, the stresses take a toll on their personal lives as well. Tommy Odds, one of their colleagues, is shot, losing his arm. After this attack, a resentful Tommy rapes the innocent Lynne, and tries to get his friends to rape her too, though they refuse. Truman does not believe Lynne's story of the rape, increasing the distance between them. In her suffering, she turns to other men and eventually leaves the South, heading to New York. Truman soon follows, but they do not live together. Their six-year-old daughter, Camara, is brutally attacked by a stranger and dies, so Truman sends for Meridian to comfort them both.

The closing section of the novel features the funeral cortege of Martin Luther King Jr., which took place in April 1968. As she marches, Meridian reconsiders the purpose of revolutionary action. In the end, both Truman and Lynne and Truman and Meridian develop platonic friendships based on shared values and Meridian recommits to political action. She emerges whole and healthy, leaving behind her fainting spells and other physical symptoms to Truman, who seems to inherit them.

As author Marge Piercy noted in her *New York Times* review of the book, "Meridian, the protagonist, is the most interesting, an attempt to make real in contemporary terms the notion of holiness and commitment. Is it possible to write a novel about the progress of a saint? Apparently, yes." Meridian may not be a saint, but she certainly embodies, politically, personally, and physically, the ambivalence of the age. Like the author who created her, she strives for authenticity and to do real good in the world, goals that are not compatible with the various ways in which she was raised. When she reaches a state of equilibrium, her health is restored and she goes into the world ready to take positive action.

Lynne, on the other hand, suffers great damage because of her good intentions. Although she loves Truman, his emotions toward her are mixed. She bears his child, suffers rape at the hands of her own colleague, lives in tremendous poverty, and eventually loses her child to violence. Although she is a child of white privilege who comes to the South seeking to discover the "authentic" black experience—something she can never do—her experiences and her tenaciousness help her transcend her early cluelessness and ignorance about the path she has chosen. Nevertheless, she never reaches the state of emotional health that Meridian does: Wracked with a racial guilt for which she can never atone, she accepts her punishment.

Truman, as a representative of black manhood in the novel, fares slightly better than many of Walker's other male protagonists. His presumptuous attitudes, however, primarily concerning Meridian and Lynne, reveal the unthinking dismissal of women's concerns, which often underlay certain aspects of the civil rights movement.

The civil rights movement itself is a major thematic element in the book. It's important to note that as Walker was composing the text, she was reconsidering many of the things it had led her to: *Meridian* was published the same year she divorced Mel Leventhal. Although it would not be prudent to read too much into that correlation, it's certainly likely that the issues of interracial relationships, the intensity of political connections, and the transitory nature of romantic love were on her mind as she wrote.

It is also in *Meridian* that we begin to see threads of Walker's sense of the spiritual richness of nature. The Sojourner, the tree at the center of the Saxon College campus, tended by the mute, otherworldly slave girl Louvinie, is one example of a natural object imbued with depth and meaning. Meridian first tries to protect the tree, then helps destroy it. Even more than that, the Sacred Serpent Mound on Meridian's family property connects the conventional world of experience to the otherworldly: it is here that Meridian first experiences her fainting spells. This theme, which becomes so important in Walker's later work, is vividly, if briefly, portrayed here.

The Temple of My Familiar

In *The Temple of My Familiar* (1989), a complex consideration of Walker's twin concerns of sexuality and spirituality, several characters from *The Color Purple* reappear briefly, and Celie's granddaughter, Fanny, is a central character. But it is the character of Miss Lissie, the elderly black female archetype, who gives the novel its philosophical meaning and creates many of its difficulties. Critic Donna Winchell has called it nothing less than "a spiritual history of the universe."

The idea of a single figure encapsulating the history of his or her people is not new: Salman Rushdie's Saleem Sinai from *Midnight's Children* and the Old Man in George Lamming's *In the Castle of My Skin* are two examples. But Walker, with her feminist and womanist concerns, connects the idea of the eternal ancestor directly to black womanhood, and Miss Lissie becomes the eternal mother ancestor, strong despite brutal attempts to crush her on the part of patriarchy and religion. She is one with the natural world—one of her alternate selves is a lioness—and with the often fraught and painful history of her people. And she is the Black Madonna, the powerful matriarch of all Christianity.

The narrative containing these big ideas is a complexly interwoven series of relationships between six characters in three shifting couples: Lissie and Hal, Carlotta and Arveyda, and Fanny and Suwelo. The female characters occupy the center of the narrative. Fanny seeks her identity through a trip to Africa and leaves her career to become a masseuse. Carlotta seeks hers through an affair with

Fanny's husband Suwelo, but discovers the emptiness of sex for its own sake, the experience that creates "two victims, both of them carting around lonely, needy bodies that were essentially blind flesh" (386). Blind flesh is explicitly contrasted with the spiritual connection that transcends ordinary human experience. In the end, Carlotta learns more about her body from Fanny's massages than from Suwelo's lovemaking. As the characters develop, they release their creative energies, painting, playwriting, building, and playing music. The ideal of unity is realized through art.

Critics have generally found *The Temple of My Familiar* to be Walker's most ambitious but least successful novel. Indeed it as much philosophical treatise as narrative, and the sermonish tone that some have identified in the text does interfere somewhat with the ability of the reader to form connections with the characters. But there is no question that Walker's goals are lofty, and that her attempt to represent all of human evolution through six residents of Northern California is a bold project.

Possessing the Secret of Joy

In *Possessing the Secret of Joy* (1992), Walker focuses on one of the minor characters from *The Color Purple*, Tashi, the Olinka girl whose commitment to remain faithful to the ways of her people even when they are damaging is so striking in the African sections of *The Color Purple*. Tashi has lost everything: her family, her village, her culture. She clings with increasing tenacity to even the most dangerous aspects of her identity, accepting the traditional Olinka custom of facial scarring toward the end of *The Color Purple*, a painful experience her partner, Celie's son Adam, chooses to share with her.

In this novel Tashi goes further: into the world of traditional female genital mutilation, a process in which the labia and clitoris of a young woman are removed and the opening to the vagina nearly closed. There is no medical reason for the procedure, but it is widely believed in traditional cultures to curb dangerous female sexuality. Tashi, engaged to Adam, undergoes the procedure by choice, as a way of demonstrating political solidarity with her people before leaving Africa for her new life in America as Evelyn Johnson. She believes that it will make her "completely woman. Completely Africa. Completely Olinka" (63). The procedure is performed by the *tsunga* M'Lissa, an elderly woman under whose knife Tashi's sister has already died.

Tashi, however, is deeply wounded by the procedure, and not just physically, though of course there are physical wounds. Adam comes and takes her to America, where they wed. Many ordinary physical processes, such as urination and menstruation, are painful and complicated for her, and their only child together is born disabled. Adam, though generally a positive character, reacts by having an affair—and a child—with Lisette, a white woman raised in Africa.

Tashi's journey from mute acceptance into madness and back to sanity comprises the core of the narrative. Her healing requires both traditional and modern psychology, including therapy with the renowned psychiatrist Carl Jung, but the most effective tool is giving herself permission to be angry at the system that assured her that this mutilation was the only way to keep their dying culture alive. Her anger centers particularly upon the *tsunga* M'Lissa, and Tashi can only really be whole by killing M'Lissa, though she is condemned to die for this act.

At her execution, her friends and family hold up a sign that explains the title of the novel. "RESISTANCE," it reads, "IS THE SECRET OF JOY!" (279). In learning to resist the mutilation practiced upon her and millions of other women, Tashi strikes an important symbolic blow against the patriarchal structures that demonize female sexuality and destroy women's lives in the name of protecting their chastity.

grandmother looked over and said, "Ooh, give me them p
pink panties you got on." Just as quick as that, Miss S
rned 'em loose, let 'em drop to the ground, and with her
ipped the panties over to Ma-Ma, who put them in her poc
grandmother looked over and said, "Ooh, give me them p
pink panties you got on." Just as quick as that, Miss S
rned 'em loose, let 'em drop to the ground, and with her
ipped the panties over to Ma-Ma, who put them in her poc
grandmother looked over and said, "Ooh, give me them p
pink panties you got on." Just as quick as that, Miss S
rned 'em loose, let 'em drop to the ground, and with her
ipped the panties over to Ma-Ma, who put them in her poc
grandmother looked over and said, "Ooh, give me them p
pink panties you got on." Just as quick as that, Miss S
rned 'em loose, let 'em drop to the ground, and with her
ipped the panties over to Ma-Ma, who put them in her poc
grandmother looked over and said, "Ooh, give me them p
pink panties you got on." Just as quick as that, Miss S
rned 'em loose, let 'em drop to the ground, and with her
ipped the panties over to Ma-Ma, who put them in her poc
grandmother looked over and said, "Ooh, give me them p
pink panties you got on." Just as quick as that, Miss S
rned 'em loose, let 'em drop to the ground, and with her
ipped the panties over to Ma-Ma, who put them in her poc
grandmother looked over and said, "Ooh, give me them p
pink panties you got on." Just as quick as that, Miss S
rned 'em loose, let 'em drop to the ground, and with her
ipped the panties over to Ma-Ma, who put them in her poc
grandmother looked over and said, "Ooh, give me them p
pink panties you got on." Just as quick as that, Miss S
rned 'em loose, let 'em drop to the ground, and with her
ipped the panties over to Ma-Ma, who put them in her poc
grandmother looked over and said, "Ooh, give me them p
pink panties you got on." Just as quick as that, Miss S
rned 'em loose, let 'em drop to the ground, and with her
ipped the panties over to Ma-Ma, who put them in her poc
grandmother looked over and said, "Ooh, give me them p
pink panties you got on." Just as quick as that, Miss S
rned 'em loose, let 'em drop to the ground, and with her

Chapter 3

Short Works

WALKER HAS ALWAYS WORKED IN SEVERAL GENRES simultaneously: poetry, novels, essays, and the short story. She
has several collections of short stories and essays, including *In Love & Trouble: Stories of Black Women* (1973),
You Can't Keep a Good Woman Down: Stories (1981), *In
Search of Our Mothers' Gardens: Womanist Prose*
(1983), and *Living By the Word: Selected Writings,
1973–87* (1988). In this section, three of her most frequently anthologized short pieces are discussed.

"Roselily" (1967)
Plot
The spare short story "Roselily" is less plot-driven than
many of Walker's works: It is composed of a stream-of-
consciousness response to the traditional marriage ceremony, and features a third-person narrator who shares
with the reader the thoughts, reflections, and responses of
the title character, a bride, during her wedding ceremony.
The ceremony itself is complete, though broken up like a
poem, phrase to phrase, set in italics, with the responses/
reflections indented, as follows:

> Dearly Beloved,
> She dreams; dragging herself across the world. A
> small girl in her mother's white robe and veil, knee
> raised waist high through a bowl of quicksand
> soup. The man who stands beside her is against
> this standing on the front porch of her house,
> being married to the sound of cars whizzing by on
> Highway 61. (3)

Analysis

Roselily is a bride, but she is not innocent. She is the mother of four children, three of whom (ages five, four, and three) are still with her. The fourth she gave to his father, a prosperous, married, Ivy League–educated civil rights worker. He lived with Roselily, but could not abide the lack of culture in the Deep South. Also, during her pregnancy, he suffered profound illnesses, as though he were the one expecting the baby. When he brought the baby to his wife, he told her he had "found the right baby through friends" (5). Her mother and grandparents have passed away, and her birth family consists of her elderly father, "a gray old man," and her younger sisters (6).

She works as a seamstress in a clothing factory, "learning to sew straight seams in workingmen's overalls, jeans, and dress pants" (7). The drudgery of the work is clear: She looks forward to her marriage if only because "[h]er place will be in the home, he has said, repeatedly, promising her rest she had prayed for" (7). But this is rest only from paid labor outside the home, not from all work. She will still have her children, and some by him as well: "They will make babies—she thinks practically about her fine brown body, his strong black one. They will be inevitable. Her hands will be full. Full of what? Babies. She is not comforted" (7). In other words, Roselily is resigned to the fact that she will be exchanging one kind of drudgery for another.

Her unnamed groom is a Black Muslim from Chicago. He offers her a way out of her small town of Panther Burn, Mississippi, out of the factory, out of poverty, and the symbolic quicksand in her yard, which threatens to suck her in. But her image of him is tied inextricably to his religion: "She thinks of the man who will be her husband, feels shut away from him because of the stiff severity of his plain black suit. His religion. A lifetime of black and white. Of veils. Covered head" (5). Though Roselily only has the vaguest notion of what a Black Muslim is, she understands that her life will change radically, even in so fundamental a matter as clothing.

One of the most controversial aspects of "Roselily" is its treatment of religion. For its "irreligious" stance, "Roselily" was banned in California in 1994. Apparently Christian, Roselily is tied equally to folk beliefs and superstition, and is marrying a Muslim. For Roselily, God is not embodied in the preacher who conducts the ceremony: "The preacher is odious to her. She wants to strike him out of the way, out of her light, with the back of her hand. It seems to her he has always been standing in front of her, barring her way." (8) If anything, "she can imagine God, a small black boy, timidly pulling the preacher's coattail" (4). Although she is not religious, she is still vaguely aware that her groom's religion sets him apart from the world she knows: "He stands curiously apart, in spite of the people crowding about to grasp his free hand. He smiles at them all but his eyes are as if turned inward. He knows they cannot understand that he is not a Christian. He will not explain himself. He feels different, he looks it" (8).

As noted elsewhere, the Black Muslim movement adhered to a strict code of behavior and demeanor, and privileged the black experience in America. Her groom's distant manner, his "difference" from the people of Panther Burn, is due primarily to his adherence to this faith, and he is proud of that difference and disdainful of Roselily in her native element. "She knows he blames Mississippi for the respectful way the men turn their heads up in the yard, the women stand waiting and knowledgeable, their children held from mischief by teachings from the wrong God" (3). In Chicago, this will change. Roselily is aware that she is a project for her new husband, that he intends to remake her in her new city.

But not, as Roselily feels, necessarily for the better. Islam, in her imagination, is "ropes, chains, handcuffs, his religion. His place of worship. Where she will be required to sit apart with covered head" (4). For her husband, life in the North as a Black Muslim is clearly preferable to the rural life they live in Panther Burn. And Roselily is prepared to believe that life in Chicago will be better in some ways. "Impatient to see the South Side, where they would live and build and be respectable and respected and free. Her husband would free her. A romantic hush. Proposal. Promises. A new life! Respectable, reclaimed, renewed. Free! In robe and veil" (7). In that last phrase, Walker critiques both the patriarchal religion and the Cinderella tradeoff to which Roselily has submitted herself. Freedom, yes, for him, and possibly her children. But the cost to her is a public and visible acceptance of her subjugated status. A common theme in Walker's work is the various paths by which blacks in her era attempted to challenge white domination. As an active member of the civil rights movement, clearly Walker was interested in this process. But too often, it denigrated or belittled the experiences of the rural poor, a wrong Walker also sought to redress in "Everyday Use."

"Everyday Use" (1973)

Plot

"Everyday Use" is presented to us as the thoughts and comments of an unnamed poor, rural black woman. She has two daughters, Dee and Maggie. Dee has always hated rural life, and has left home to get an education, paid for largely by the community, in the outside world. Maggie, scarred over much of her body from a house fire, has stayed home with her mother. She appears to be developmentally delayed and is often afraid, rarely speaking or raising her eyes. Nevertheless she adheres to the old country ways and has a suitor, John Thomas, whom she expects to marry. The story is set during a visit Dee makes to her old home.

Women Writers
Texts and Contexts

"Everyday Use"

ALICE WALKER

*Edited
and with an
introduction by*
BARBARA T.
CHRISTIAN

IN "EVERYDAY USE," WALKER CONFRONTS THE VERY CORE OF
THE IDENTITY CONFLICT EXPERIENCED BY GENERATIONS OF
AFRICAN AMERICANS.

The narrator and Maggie prepare for Dee's arrival. They wait outside, and the narrator thinks of television shows in which parents and their successful children are reunited by surprise, then realizes that Dee will never be delighted to see her in that way. When Dee arrives, she is dressed in a colorful caftan and has her hair done in a complex pattern. She instructs her mother and sister to call her Wangero Leewanika Kemanjo, explaining that Dee is dead: "I couldn't bear it any longer, being named after the people who oppress me" (53). To her mother's observation that she was named after a favorite aunt who was in turn named after her own mother, Dee/Wangero shows no interest.

The man who accompanies her, whom the narrator calls Asalamalakim after the Arabic greeting that is the first thing he says to her, is similarly outlandish to her country eyes: "Hair is all over his head a foot long and hanging from his chin like a kinky mule tail" (52). His name, she says, is "twice as long and three times as hard" (54) as her daughter's, so they settle on the less-complicated "Hakim-a-barber." The narrator is not informed of their relationship, nor does she ask.

The primary purpose of Dee/Wangero's visit seems to be to comb her childhood home for rustic artifacts: a butter dish, a churn, quilts. Her interest in these items is anthropological: certainly she has no interest in putting them to "everyday use."

The climax of the story occurs when Dee/Wangero, who rejected her mother's offer of a quilt when she went to college as "old-fashioned, out of style," now demands several quilts peremptorily.

The mother, who does not completely understand her daughter, but certainly understands the gross disrespect she exudes, refuses to give her the quilts, which have already been promised to Maggie when she marries.

> Dee (Wangero) looked at me with hatred. "You just will not understand. The point is these quilts, *these* quilts!"
> "Well," I said, stumped. "What would you do with them?"
> "Hang them," she said. As if that was the only thing you *could* do with quilts. (58)

Despite Maggie's willingness to defer to her sister (as her mother notes, "She thinks her sister has held life always in the palm of one hand, that 'no' is a word the world never learned to say to her" (47)), the mother refuses to give up the quilts, literally ripping them out of "Miss Wangero's hands" and bestowing them upon the younger sister, the damaged daughter who insists that she can "'member Grandma Dee without the quilts," the one who will put them to "everyday use" (58).

Dee/Wangero is furious at this development, insisting that her mother "just [doesn't] understand."

> "What don't I understand?" I wanted to know.
> "Your heritage," she said. (59)

As Wangero and Hakim-the-barber drive away, Maggie smiles.

Analysis

In this story Walker takes aim at a certain kind of black American identity that sought to escape its own origins, or rather, jump over them back to Africa. Wangero, with her impossible African name, complicated hair, and dress "so loud it hurts my eyes" (52), has eagerly and rudely cut her ties to her poor, rural past. Her mother has long known of her distaste for their lifestyle: A decade earlier, when their old house burned to the ground (the fire in which Maggie received her scars) the mother recalls: "And Dee. I see her standing off under the sweet gum tree she used to dig gum out of; a look of concentration on her face as she watched the last dingy gray board of the house fall in toward the red-hot brick chimney. Why don't you do a dance around the ashes? I'd wanted to ask her. She had hated the house that much" (49–50). Her tastes were always different from her family's: beautiful rather than practical. The mother who wears "flannel nightgowns to bed and overalls during the day" (48) has raised a daughter who demands "a yellow organdy dress to wear to her graduation" (50). But the difference between Dee and her mother and sister is not one of mere aesthetics: She openly disdains them. "She wrote me once that wherever we 'choose' to live, she will manage to come and see us. But she will never bring her friends" (51).

With a renewed racial consciousness, however, the objects in her family home have gained prestige. Dee/Wangero thrills at the rump marks left in a bench her father made, at the top of a butter churn, not because they are useful (and actively in use by the mother and Maggie), but because they are historic, rustic. She does not value the people themselves: her mother and sister, her father, her grandmother, the aunt after whom she is named. She is not interested in personal tribute, but in material objects. Butter dishes have replaced organdy dresses as the objects of her desire.

Her mother, however, takes a stand. With a feeling that "something hit me in the top of my head and ran down to the soles of my feet" (58), she resists the transformation of her small farmhouse from dingy shack to anthropological candy store. She insists on Maggie's rights in the face of an older daughter who believes that they should be grateful that she even wants their possessions. In this moment, Walker articulates clearly her allegiance to her own rural past as something real, not as a passing fashion for hip Africanists.

One other central image should be noted here: the specific object that Dee/Wangero chooses as the battleground. Quilting as American (and here specifically African-American) folk art is an important symbol throughout Walker's work. Taking the scraps of history, piecing them together into something beautiful and useful, is an act of artistic creation. "*These* quilts" are the ones deemed "priceless" by the daughter who desires them. They are withheld for the daughter who actually remembers their origin and will use them in her home, the daughter who represents continuity with the past.

"Beauty: When the Other Dancer Is the Self" (1983)

In this nonfiction memoir/essay, Walker ruminates on the injury she suffered at the age of eight that radically changed her sense of herself and the world. Walker was a lively and intelligent child, but at the age of eight, while playing with her brothers, she was the victim of an unfortunate accident: One of her brothers shot her in the eye with a BB gun. The accident was compounded, however, by her brothers' injunction to silence, by a hastily crafted lie that covered their tracks but blinded the young Alice in one eye.

> "If you tell," they say, "we will get a whipping. You don't want that to happen, do you?" I do not. "Here is a piece of wire," says the older brother, picking it up from the roof; "say you stepped on one end of it and the other flew up and hit you." . . . If I do not say this is what happened, I know my brothers will find ways to make me wish I had. But now I will say anything that gets me to my mother. (386–387)

Untreated, the eye develops an infection. Although her parents try to flag down a ride to a doctor that day, the white motorist they stop refuses to help. It is a week, then, before Walker sees a doctor, and the doctor chastises her parents for their negligence. Then he utters the words that terrify the young Walker: "'Eyes are sympathetic,' he says. 'If one is blind, the other will likely become blind too.'"

So the trauma of the injury begins to compound: first the injury itself (which Walker blames on gender bias: her brothers, being boys, got guns and she did not), then the blindness, then the fear that she might lose her sight entirely.

And then the scar: "But it is really how I look that bothers me most. Where the BB pellet struck there is a glob of whitish scar tissue, a hideous cataract, on my eye. Now when I stare at people—a favorite pastime, up to now—they will stare back. Not at the 'cute' little girl but at her scar. For six years I do not stare at anyone because I do not raise my head" (387).

The family had recently moved, and the new school, a former prison, terrified young Walker. Her parents, in an attempt to provide her with some stability, sent her back to her old school, which meant living with her grandparents. Walker interprets this as rejection, as punishment. The trauma is compounded yet again when her mother falls ill and she is only allowed a brief visit: "The weeks pass but I am hardly aware of it. All I know is that my mother might die, my father is not so jolly, my brothers still have their guns, and I am the one sent away from home" (389).

The trauma is clearly unbearable for a child who is not yet nine, but she fixes all her anger on her eye, which for years symbolized the injustices and dislocations of this period. "That night, as I do almost every night, I abuse my eye. I rant and rave at it, in front of the mirror. I plead with it to clear up before morning. I tell it I hate and despise it. I do not pray for sight. I pray for beauty" (389).

Least understandable of all to Walker, writing as an adult, is the insistence of her mother and her sister that she "did not change" during this period, which she recalls as dramatically transformative.

> Years later, in the throes of a mid-life crisis I asked my mother and sister whether I changed after the "accident." "No," they say, puzzled. "What do you mean?"
> What do I mean? (387)
> . . .
> "You did not change," they say.
> *Did I imagine the anguish of never looking up?* (389)
> . . .
> "You did not change," they say. (389)

At age fourteen, Walker visits her brother in Boston and he arranges to have the scar tissue removed. "There is still a small bluish crater where the scar tissue was, but the ugly white stuff is gone. Almost immediately I become a different person from the girl who does not raise her head. Or so I think" (389–390). Restored to beauty, if not sight, she regains her confidence and begins to excel again.

A photo shoot for a magazine, however, precipitates a crisis in her self-image: she fears that the blind eye, which has a tendency to wander (that is, not stay in line with the seeing eye) will show on the magazine cover, particularly if she does not get enough sleep.

> At night in bed with my lover I think up reasons why I should not appear on the cover of a magazine. "My meanest critics will say I've sold out," I say. "My family will now realize I write scandalous books."
> "But what's the real reason you don't want to do this?" he asks.

"Because in all probability," I say in a rush, "my eye won't be straight."

"It will be straight enough," he says. Then, "Besides, I thought you'd made your peace with that."

And I suddenly remember that I have. (390–391)

The final "scene" in the essay features Walker's young daughter Rebecca studying the remaining scar tissue. Looking at the bluish scar, she observes, "Mommy, there's a *world* in your eye!" (393). Walker takes the child's comment seriously, and it changes her whole sense of self: "There was a world in my eye. And I saw that it was possible to love it: that in fact, for all it had taught me of shame and anger and inner vision, I did love it. Even to see it drifting out of orbit in boredom, or rolling up out of fatigue, not to mention floating back at attention in excitement (bearing witness, a friend has called it), deeply suitable to my personality, and even characteristic of me" (393). She sees herself as a dancer, dancing with her perfect self: "She is beautiful, whole, and free. And she is also me" (393).

As an extended rumination on the nature of seeing and being seen, "Beauty" is a compelling essay. But it works on other levels as well. One important thread is the casual cruelty of family life: the fact that Walker's brothers made their blamelessness a precondition for getting their injured sister help, for example, or the invisibility of the young girl's emotional trauma to those closest to her.

Ultimately "Beauty" fits smoothly into Walker's body of work. Yes, the essay argues, it does matter how and whether people see us, but what matters more is love of self, love of the world. In reframing her trauma to bring her whole and injured selves together, Walker creates a model for moving forward from pain without denying its power, for making it part of yourself without making it the only part of yourself. It is a potent and valuable lesson.

In these short works, Walker develops her most important ideas in concise form: Relationships between men and women, between women and women, between members of a family are all examined. The dense symbolism of the quilt, of the scar, points to her larger concerns, and the importance of finding beauty in damage resonates through all these stories.

Works

Novels
1970 *The Third Life of Grange Copeland*
1976 *Meridian*
1982 *The Color Purple*
1989 *The Temple of My Familiar*
1992 *Possessing the Secret of Joy*
1998 *By the Light of My Father's Smile*
2005 *Now Is the Time to Open Your Heart*

Short Story Collections
1973 *In Love & Trouble: Stories of Black Women*
1981 *You Can't Keep a Good Woman Down: Stories*
1994 *To Hell With Dying*
2005 *The Complete Stories*
1996 *Banned*
2000 *The Way Forward Is with a Broken Heart*
2006 *There Is a Flower at the Tip of My Nose Smelling Me*

Poetic Works
1968 *Once*
1973 *Revolutionary Petunias and Other Poems*
1979 *Goodnight, Willie Lee, I'll See You in the Morning*
1984 *Horses Make the Landscape Look More Beautiful*
1991 *Her Blue Body Everything We Know: Earthling Poems, 1965–1990 Complete*
2003 *Absolute Trust in the Goodness of the Earth*
2003 *A Poem Traveled Down My Arm*

Essays

1983   *In Search of Our Mothers' Gardens: Womanist Prose*

1988   *Living By the Word: Selected Writings, 1973–87*

1993   *Warrior Marks: Female Genital Mutilation and the Sexual Binding of Women* (with Pratibha Parmar)

1996   *The Same River Twice: Honoring the Difficult: A Meditation on Life, Spirit, Art, and the Making of the Film* The Color Purple, *Ten Years Later*

1997   *Anything We Love Can Be Saved: A Writer's Activism*

2001   *Sent by Earth: A Message from the Grandmother Spirit after the Attacks on the World Trade Center and the Pentagon*

2006   *We Are the Ones We Have Been Waiting For: Inner Light in a Time of Darkness*

Edited Readers

1974   *Langston Hughes, American Poet*

1979   *I Love Myself When I'm Laughing . . . and Then Again When I Am Looking Mean and Impressive: A Zora Neale Hurston Reader*

Filmography

1977   *Diary of an African Nun*. Directed by Julie Dash. Starring Barbara O. Jones. Independent.

1985   *The Color Purple*. Directed by Steven Spielberg. Produced by Quincy Jones and Peter Guber. Screenplay by Menno Meyjes. Starring Whoopi Goldberg, Danny Glover, Margaret Avery, and Oprah Winfrey. Warner Brothers.

2003   *Everyday Use*. Directed by Bruce Schwartz. Starring Karen ffolkes, Rachel Luttrell, Lyne Odums, and Gary Poux. Films for the Humanities and Sciences.

Chronology

1944

February 9: Alice Malsenior Walker born in Eatonton, Georgia.

1952

Summer: Loses sight in right eye after being shot in a BB gun accident.

1958

Summer: Spends summer in Boston. Undergoes surgery to remove scar tissue from eye.

1961 Graduates from high school as valedictorian. Starts Spelman College in Atlanta.

1963 Howard Zinn summarily dismissed from Spelman. Walker writes to student newspaper to protest.

1964

January: Starts Sarah Lawrence College in Bronxville, New York. Meets Muriel Rukeyser.

1965 Spends summer in Georgia, registering voters, then in Africa. Gets pregnant, has abortion.

1966
January: Graduates from Sarah Lawrence. Goes to
               work for New York City Welfare
               Department, then leaves to work with the
               NAACP in Mississippi. Meets Mel
               Leventhal.

1967
March 17:   Marries Melvyn Rosenmann Leventhal in
               New York.

1968   *Once* (book of poetry) published.

1969
November 17:   Daughter Rebecca Grant Leventhal born.

1970   *The Third Life of Grange Copeland*
               (novel) published.
               Receives Radcliffe Fellowship, moves to
               Cambridge, with daughter Rebecca.

1973   *Revolutionary Petunias* (poems) pub-
               lished. *In Love & Trouble* (short stories)
               published.

January 26:   Willie Lee Walker, Alice's father, dies.

August 15:   Walker locates grave of Zora Neale
               Hurston in Fort Pierce, Florida.

1974   Moves to New York City with Rebecca
               and Mel Leventhal.

1976   Divorces Mel Leventhal.
               Meridian (novel) published.

1978   Moves to California.

1979   *Good Night Willie Lee, I'll See You in the Morning* (poetry) published. *I Love Myself When I Am Laughing . . . and Then Again When I Am Looking Mean and Impressive* (edited anthology) published.

1981   *You Can't Keep a Good Woman Down* (short stories) published.

1982   *The Color Purple* (novel) published.

1983   Wins Pulitzer Prize for *The Color Purple*. *In Search of Our Mothers' Gardens* (essays) published.

1984   Wild Trees Press started. *Horses Make a Landscape Look More Beautiful* (poetry) published.

1985   Film version of *The Color Purple*, directed by Steven Spielberg, released.

1986   *The Color Purple* is nominated for eleven Oscars.

1988   *To Hell with Dying* (children's book) published. *Living by the Word* (essays) published.

1989   *The Temple of My Familiar* (novel) published.

1991	*Her Blue Body Everything We Know: Earthling Poems, 1965–1990 Complete* (poems) published.
1992	*Possessing the Secret of Joy* (novel) published.
1993	*Warrior Marks* (screenplay) released. Minnie Lou Walker dies.
1994	*The Complete Stories* (short stories) published. Changes name to Alice Tallulah-Kate Walker.
1996	*The Same River Twice: Honoring the Difficult* (memoir) published.
1997	*Anything We Love Can Be Saved* (essays) published. Named Humanist of the Year by the American Humanist Association.
1998	*By the Light of My Father's Smile* (novel) published.
2000	*The Way Forward Is with a Broken Heart* (short stories/memoir) published. Rebecca Leventhal Walker's *Black, White, and Jewish: Autobiography of a Shifting Self* (memoir) published.
2001	*Sent by Earth: A Message from the Grandmother Spirit after the Attacks on the World Trade Center and the Pentagon* (essay) delivered as speech and published.

2003   *Absolute Trust in the Goodness of the Earth* (poetry) published.
        A Poem Traveled Down My Arm (poetry) published.

2004   *Now Is the Time to Open Your Heart* (novel) published.

2006   Inducted into the California Hall of Fame by Governor Arnold Schwarzenegger.
        There Is a Flower at the Tip of My Nose Smelling Me (children's book; illustrations by Stefano Vitale) published.
        We Are the Ones We Have Been Waiting For: Inner Light in a Time of Darkness (essays) published.

Notes

Part I: Chapter 1

p. 13, par. 3, "About their allegation that she too, had been a 'gun-wielding cowboy,' half a century later, Alice would defend herself as she had not been able to do as an eight-year-old girl with a wounded eye: 'My instinct is that my brothers have concocted another face-saving story. Again, it is their word against mine. If I had a gun, too, the battle would seem fair.'" Evelyn C. White, *Alice Walker: A Life*, (New York: Norton, 2004), p. 40.

p. 37, par. 1, Walker's advocacy on behalf of Hurston earned her a fair amount of press and precipitated a falling out with Muriel Rukeyser, her former mentor, who had known Hurston in the 1930s. A series of bitter letters passed between Rukeyser and her former student, but the last, in which Rukeyser stated that "my wishes and my love for you and your work are unchanged," and hinted that she had played some role in Walker's abortion, was unsent at the time of her death. Evelyn C. White, *Alice Walker: A Life*, (New York: Norton, 2004), pp. 274–275.

p. 43, par. 3–p. 44, par. 1, Zora Neale Hurston, "Dedication: On Refusing to be Humbled by Second Place in a Contest You Did Not Design," in *I Love Myself When I Am Laughing . . . and Then Again When I Am Looking Mean and Impressive*, ed. Alice Walker (New York: Feminist Press, 1980).

p. 46, par. 1, Rebecca Walker, "How My Mother's Fanatical Views Tore Us Apart," *Mail Online*, May 23, 2008, http://www.dailymail.co.uk/femail/article-1021293/

How-mothers-fanatical-feminist-views-tore-apart-daughter-The-Color-Purple-author.html (accessed August 12, 2008).

Part I: Chapter 2

p. 50, par. 1, John Strausbaugh, *Black Like You: Blackface, Whiteface, Insult and Imitation in American Popular Culture*, (New York: Tarcher/Penguin, 2006).

p. 61, par. 2, Interview with Chris Albertson, *JerryJazzMusician*, September 22, 2003, http://www.jerry-jazzmusician.com/mainHTML.cfm?page=albertson.html (accessed July 1, 2008).

p. 68, par. 2, In later years, Baraka became an increasingly controversial figure, speaking out against homosexuals, Jews, and women; the same energy that allowed him to be such an impassioned defender of his movement also seemed to function as a set of blinders, preventing him from seeing the prejudices faced by others. He played a prominent role, for example, in the attacks on *The Color Purple*.

Part II: Chapter 1

p. 81, par. 2, Alice Walker, *The Color Purple* (New York: Harvest/Harcourt, 2003). All citations are to this edition.

p. 99, par. 3, "It's probably a cinch that if Mr. Spielberg hadn't been attracted to Miss Walker's novel, nobody else would have touched it. We've come a long way, babies, but not quite far enough so that an immensely popular book about black life would have prompted a scramble among movie people to acquire the screen rights. . . . Miss Walker's 'Color Purple' is something else—a grim, rudely funny, black-feminist family chronicle, set in the deep South, with not a decent white person in sight. It could only have been gotten onto the screen by Mr. Spielberg, backed as he is by his phenomenal record of box-office hits: 'Jaws,' 'Close Encounters of the Third Kind,' 'Raiders of the Lost Ark,' 'Poltergeist,' 'Gremlins,' 'E.T.' and 'Indiana Jones and the Temple of Doom.'" Mel Watkins, "Some Letters Went to God," *New York Times*, July 25, 1982, http://www.nytimes.com/books/ 98/10/04/ specials/walker-color.html (accessed December 5, 2008).

p. 100, par. 1, Vincent Canby, "Film View: For a Palette of Cliches Come 'The Color Purple,'" *New York Times*, January 5, 1986.

p. 103, par. 1, Earl Walter, Jr. to Quincy Jones *See* Alice Walker, *The Same River Twice. Honoring the Difficult*, (New York: Wheeler Publishing, 1996).

Further Information

Books

Bates, Gerri. *Alice Walker: A Critical Companion.* Westport, CT: Greenwood, 2005.

Lauret, Maria. *Alice Walker.* New York: St. Martin's Press, 2000.

Simcikova, Karla. *To Live Fully Here and Now: The Healing Vision in the Works of Alice Walker.* Lanham, MD: Lexington, 2007.

White, Evelyn C. *Alice Walker: A Life.* New York: Norton, 2004.

Websites

http://www.womenshistory.about.com/od/alicewalker/a/alice_walker.htm
About Alice Walker at About.com: Women's History

http://www.luminarium.org/contemporary/alicew/
Anniina's Alice Walker Page

http://www.novelguide.com/thecolorpurple/index.html
"The Color Purple" Novelguide.com

http://www.pbs.org/wgbh/amex/eyesontheprize/
Eyes on the Prize: America's Civil Rights Movement 1954–1985

http://www.gale.cengage.com/free_resources/bhm/bio/walker_a.htm
The Gale Group. "Alice Walker"

http://www.uga.edu/~womanist/
Womanist Theory and Research. University of Georgia, Womanist Studies Consortium

Bibliography

All citations to Walker's writing in the text come from the works listed in this bibliography.

"Alabama Removes Ban on Interracial Marriage." *USA Today*, November 7, 2000. http://www.usatoday.com/news/vote2000/al/main03.htm (accessed July 10, 2008).

Albertson, Christ. "Radio Interview by Bessie Smith." *WHAT Philadelphia* (1958).

Banks, Erma D., and Keith Byerman. *Alice Walker: An Annotated Bibliography*. New York: Garland, 1989.

Bloom, Harold. *Alice Walker*. In *Bloom's Major Authors Collection* by Harold Bloom. Philadelphia: Chelsea House Publishers, 1999.

Bobo, Jacqueline. "Black Women's Responses to *The Color Purple*." *Jump Cut* 33 (February 1988): 43–51.

Brunner, Borgna, and Elissa Haney. "Timeline of the Civil Rights Movement." *Information Please*, 2007. http://www.infoplease.com/spot/civilrightstimeline1.html (accessed July 10, 2008).

Canby, Vincent. "Film View: For a Palette of Cliches Come 'The Color Purple.'" *New York Times*, January 5, 1986.

Davis, Ronald L. F., "Creating Jim Crow: In-Depth Essay." *The History of Jim Crow.* http://www.jimcrowhistory.org/history/creating2.htm (accessed June 27, 2008).

Dworkin, Susan. "The Strange and Wonderful Story of the Making of *The Color Purple*," *Ms.* magazine, December 1985. Reprinted in Alice Walker. *The Same River Twice: Honoring the Difficult*. New York: Wheeler Publishing, 1996.

Eyes on the Prize: The Civil Rights Movement in America, 1955–1985, "Project 'C' in Birmingham" PBS television (1987), http://www.pbs.org/wgbh/amex/eyesontheprize/story/07_c.html (accessed October 11, 2008).

Farmer, Jim. "Color Me with Potential." Review of *The Color Purple*, adapted by Marsha Norman, directed by Gary Griffin, Atlanta. *The Southern Voice*, September 24, 2004. http://www.sovo.com/2004/9-24/arts/theater/color.cfm (accessed December 5, 2008).

Freeman, Ronald L. *A Communion of Spirits: African American Quilters, Preservers and Their Stories*. Nashville: Rutledge Hill Press, 1996.

Hentoff, Nat, and Nat Shapiro. *Hear Me Talkin' to Ya: The Story of Jazz as Told by the Men Who Made It*. New York: Dover, 1966.

Lauret, Maria. *Alice Walker*. Modern Novelists Series. New York: St. Martin's Press, 2000.

Levine, Lawrence W. *Black Culture and Black Consciousness*. Oxford, England: Oxford University Press, 1977.

O'Brien, John, ed. *Interviews with Black Writers*. New York: Liveright, 1973.

Piercy, Marge. "Meridian." Review of *Meridian* by Alice Walker. *The New York Times*, May 23, 1976. http://www.nytimes.com/books/98/10/04/specials/walker-meridian.html (accessed June 24, 2008).

Strausbaugh, John. *Black Like You: Blackface, Whiteface, Insult and Imitation in American Popular Culture*. New York: Tarcher/Penguin, 2006.

Walker, Alice. "Beauty: When the Other Dancer Is the Self." From *In Search of Our Mother's Gardens: Womanist Prose*. New York: Harvest/Harcourt, 2003.

_____. *The Color Purple*. New York: Harvest/Harcourt 2003.

_____. "Dedication: On Refusing to be Humbled by Second Place in a Contest You Did Not Design." From Zora Neale Hurston, *I Love Myself When I Am Laughing . . . and Then Again When I am Looking Mean and Impressive*, ed. Alice Walker. New York: Feminist Press, 1980.

_____. "Everyday Use." *Women Writers: Texts and Contexts*. Ed. Barbara T. Christian. New Brunswick, NJ: Rutgers University Press, 1994.

_____. *In Love & Trouble: Stories of Black Women*. New York: Harcourt, 1973.

Walker, Rebecca Leventhal. *Black, White, and Jewish: Autobiography of a Shifting Self*. New York: Riverhead, 2001.

_____. "How My Mother's Fanatical Views Tore Us Apart," *Mail Online*, May 23, 2008. http://www.daily-mail.co.uk/ femail/article-1021293/How-mothers-fanatical-feminist-views-tore-apart-daughter-The-Color-Purple-author.html (accessed August 12, 2008).

Wallace, Michele. "Blues for Mr. Spielberg." *The Village Voice*, March 18, 1986, 27.

White, Evelyn C. *Alice Walker: A Life*. New York: Norton, 2004.

Winchell, Donna Haisty. *Alice Walker*. Twayne's United States Authors Series Online. New York: G.K. Hall & Co., 1999.

Zinn, Howard. *You Can't Be Neutral on a Moving Train: A Personal History of Our Times*. Boston: Beacon, 1994.

Index

Page numbers in **boldface** are illustrations, tables, and charts. Proper names of fictional characters are shown by (C).

About the Author

MARY DONNELLY is an assistant professor of English at Broome Community College in Binghamton, New York. She received her doctorate at the University of Miami, Coral Gables, Florida. She lives in upstate New York with her spouse and four children. This is her first book for Marshall Cavendish Benchmark.